THE OFFBEAT SARI

Edited by Priya Khanchandani

the
DESIGN
MUSEUM

HALF TITLE   Raw Mango, Avium Sari, Other collection, 2021
TITLE PAGE   Ekaya (Revival Project), hand-woven Blue Tissue
                Zari Sari (right) and hand-woven Blue Zari Sari
                with floral motif (left), 2021

Director's Foreword

Tim Marlow

The Offbeat Sari looks at the ways in which the sari has experienced a radical twenty-first-century overhaul. The first large-scale exhibition in the UK to focus on the sari as a fashion garment in India today, it brings together more than ninety examples of trailblazing saris made over the past decade, nearly all of which are on loan from designers and studios in India and haven't been displayed in this country before. This book – published in parallel with the exhibition – hones in on some of the most intriguing stories of designers, wearers and craftspeople shaping the sari. Through the lens of their creativity, it presents a snapshot of the fashion revolution the sari is now experiencing, predominantly in urban India.

The sari, recognised around the world and ubiquitous across South Asia, is little understood internationally in its contemporary form. Its renewed popularity is one of today's most important global fashion stories, yet it has rarely been touched on within global conversation. The insertion of India into a global design aesthetic has, in the words of art historian Saloni Mathur, 'concealed a broader, 150-year-old complex of meanings generated by the encounter of Indian culture with the west'.[1] Those encounters and, in turn, our understanding of Indian design globally have been shaped by the specific perspectives generated by centuries of colonial rule. Contemporary displays of Indian design have been known to hark back to stereotypical definitions of India, while the demands of consumerism have positioned India in terms of established design tropes such as paisley or henna. Within museums, exhibitions on South Asia have inevitably been shaped by collections that form part of the foundations of imperialism, and tend to draw attention to timelessness at the expense of progress.

The Design Museum examines the world as it is today from the perspective of design. We are conscious of our legacy as a museum – including the fact that we have never staged an exhibition dedicated to South Asia before – and of the need to redefine our representation of contemporary design by presenting the work of designers across geographies. *The Offbeat Sari* will highlight design's role in a huge fashion story, providing a site for us to reflect – along with our partners and lenders in India, and the South Asian diaspora here – on the ingenuity of Indian textiles within the context of cutting-edge fashion. We will see that innovation can be driven by fashion brands, but it can also be driven by street culture, activists and individual makers. In each case, design plays a critical role.

The Design Museum would like to thank lenders and other participants for their generous support in helping us to realise this project, and for enabling us to tell the story of a dynamic object that plays such a crucial part in the everyday lives of people. As the story of objects goes, the sari offers an extraordinary insight into the social, economic and creative context of a burgeoning nation.

1   Saloni Mathur, *India by Design:
    Colonial History and Cultural
    Display* (Oakland, CA: University
    of California Press, 2007), 5.

Introduction

Priya Khanchandani

Attempting to define the sari in these pages might seem outrageous. After all, the richness of its texture, the detail of its surface, the voluptuousness of its architecture and the depth of its history defy easy delineation, eluding the grasp of language. Still, something needs to be said of its present incarnation. Woven from steel, stitched from hand-distressed denim, knotted, pleated or belted; worn in protest, celebration or even on the daily commute – today's sari is in the throes of a reinvention. Its millennia-old structure and style are being remade with imagination and creativity, reshaping the meaning of fashion in contemporary India. Its symbolism continues to shift with this revolution, giving voice at its most avant-garde to marginalised perspectives and subverting conventions of femininity.

This book – and the exhibition I curated alongside it at the Design Museum in London – cannot claim to encompass the sari's infinite guises. Nor can it do justice to its vast geographical scope across South Asia, including Bangladesh, where there is a rich tradition of textile craft that has shaped the sari across the subcontinent. Instead, what it sets out to do is describe the particular ways in which the sari has become a site for design innovation, enabling the expression of new identities and materialities, primarily in the context of urban India today. It documents how the sari has slipped beyond the boundaries of convention in unexpected ways and been reborn in its most 'offbeat' form – the 'offbeat' sari being the sari as imagined in the last decade or so for a diverse, contemporary world by Indian designers, wearers and makers.

The sari's origins go back as far as the Indus Valley Civilisation, when cotton was first cultivated and natural dyes – turmeric, indigo and lac – enlivened it with colour. Notwithstanding its ancient origins, the sari's basic form remains largely intact. Perhaps for this reason, the sari is often understood internationally as being 'timeless' – despite such a term failing to acknowledge its capacity to evolve, its fluidity and its sustained contemporaneity – characteristics that are still boldly evident today.

In the most literal sense, the sari might be defined as a garment composed of a piece of unstitched cloth, most commonly nine yards long (8.2 metres) but starting at anything from around 3.5 yards (3.2 metres). Different densities of weave across the sari help it to take shape when draped across the body in styles that reflect regional variation, practicality and personal preference. The most common way of wearing the sari is the classical Nivi drape, which was popularised in the 1870s by Jnanadanandini Devi, a member of the prominent Tagore family. The sari is wrapped around the waist, then pleated at the front and tucked into the waistband of a petticoat, with the loose end of the fabric, called the pallu, worn across the torso and draped over the left shoulder.

But the sari is more than a garment, or a length of cloth. It is a vessel for communicating shifting notions of female identity, a language expressed through fabric, an ideology that has evolved over time with the changing contours of the cultural landscape. Unlike a pre-stitched garment, its form is shaped by its wearer; the wearer's experience of embodying it lends the sari not only shape but also meaning. The way in which the sari falls over the body alters the sensation of wearing it, and this interaction is crucial to its wider definition: the places where the flesh meets the cloth, where the pallu falls over the shoulder and needs to be held by the arm, the point where the pleats are tucked into the waist or the way the sari moves with a gesture or a footstep.

Jnanadanandini Devi, Satyendranath Tagore, Kadambari Devi and Jyotirindranath Tagore, 1897

In the March 2022 issue of *Vogue India*, with the sari's renaissance well under way, journalist Bandana Tewari reflected on how the sari was tamed by the politics of colonialism in the nineteenth century, homogenising its form and determining that it be worn with a blouse and petticoat:

> History has shown us that often times, the chastity of women has been smeared on the promiscuity of the sari. With the British colonisation of India in the 19th century began the colonisation of the female body. Till that point, saris were wrapped sinuously around the body – one piece of translucent fabulousness without any undergarments. But to the colonisers, exposure of the body was a marker of savagery, tribalism and obscenity. A pity indeed, as a living, breathing cloth that was replete with the symbolism of an untameable spirit and the ferocity of feminine energy, was stripped in the name of sartorial morality.[1]

The idea of the sari, then, became wrapped up in the politics of Britain's colonial mission, which aimed not only to conquer but also to infiltrate, repositioning Indian culture in terms of an acutely Western gaze. Textiles were colonised not only at a cultural but also an economic level through a vast monopoly on production imposed by the East India Company, which entailed Britain exporting India's raw cotton, turning it into cheap textiles using British power looms, before selling it across Europe – and back to India. In reaction to the injustice of this arrangement, and to India's state of oppression more broadly, Mahatma Gandhi famously initiated sustained opposition to British cloth, tapping into interest in hand-loom weaving from British officials such as EB Havell and the first generation of Indian art critics like Ananda Coomaraswamy. The Swadeshi campaign, as it was known, boycotted British cloth and propagated hand-spun, hand-woven cotton – or khadi – as being synonymous on a metaphorical level with Indian nationalism.[2] Encouraging individuals to spin their own fabric in an act of self-determination diluted the nation's reliance on Britain's industrially produced equivalent, simultaneously undermining the chokehold of colonial power on Indian textile-making.

Since India attained independence in 1947, the sari has become a screen on to which India's 'modern' identity could project its nascent form, drawing on the ideological legacy of cloth that had already been established and which had evolved along with the subcontinent's shifting state of affairs. The evolution of the contemporary sari returns us to the founding principles of Indian design, devised post-independence and intertwined with postcolonial ideologies.

The 'idea of India' devised by India's first prime minister, Jawaharlal Nehru, conceived of a modern, industrialised nation articulated through the functionality and technology afforded by modernist design. Before this, during the nationalist movement, an appreciation for craft had taken root in the form of the Swadeshi movement promoted by Gandhi and had been continued by intellectuals such as Pupul Jayakar, the writer on Indian craft and founder of the Handicrafts and Handlooms Export Corporation of India. The threads of these competing ideas – industrialisation on the one hand and craft on the other – became the foundations of an emergent design language for modern India. They were reflected in the ethos of a new establishment, the National Institute of Design. Founded in 1961 as the National Institute of Industrial Design, this was India's first university dedicated to a design consciousness that bridged tradition and modernity. Its newly devised curriculum was based on The India Report – compiled in 1958 by American designers Charles and Ray Eames, who were invited by the Indian government to research

PM Dalwadi, 1964. Construction of the National Institute of Design building, Ahmedabad, India

design across the country, meeting writers, craftspeople, architects, industrialists, educators and others to aid them in developing a formal programme of design training.

In the decades that followed, shifting attitudes led to the emergence of neoliberal aspirations in India, resulting in the liberalisation of its economy in 1991. The 'idea of India' upon which the nation had been founded was tested by the influx of foreign investment, and the infiltration of India's borders by a quintessentially American brand of globalisation. As economic prosperity followed, India became the fourth largest global economy. A rising middle class began to emerge in tandem with new sites appearing across India's burgeoning cities, a shift that was characterised by the privatisation of public space and the rapid rise of new consumer destinations, including fashion boutiques. These new spatial genres expressed a visual language that was quite distinct from the India of an earlier era. They departed from modernist principles in favour of an international style characterised by glass and steel, with more ample leisure spaces conducive to consumption, often segregated along socioeconomic lines. New luxury malls and shopping districts provided fertile ground for fashion designers hoping to reach consumers.

Against the backdrop of shifting social norms throughout the 1980s to the early 2000s, the popularity of the sari waned in favour of alternative forms of dress, with women gravitating towards Western clothing and the salwar kameez, comprising loose trousers and a tunic. The erosion of the sari's regional diversity and the homogenisation of the Nivi drape as the 'standard' has also been given as a reason for the sari's lull.[3] By 1990, *India Today* was reporting that the sari was considered by many as 'staid, standard and almost sacred'.[4] It had become associated with an unfashionable older generation, or was confined to occasion wear, and it was viewed by many younger people as contrived and uncomfortable. Stereotypical depictions in Bollywood cinema – the unravelling of the sari, or the wet sari worn by a female protagonist – fetishised the female body in ways that felt out of tune with the aspirations of professional women.

The rapid industrialisation of textile production led to the rise of the synthetic sari, made on a power loom, and, as fashion (in parallel with architecture) shifted away from the twin principles of craft and modernism, the hand-loom sari was further relegated to the realms of tradition. At the same time, a smaller movement was taking hold in intellectual circles, its seeds sown by an earlier generation who retained a strong appreciation for craft. Such groups were inspired by powerful women from history like Indira Gandhi, the first female prime minister of India, who wore khadi saris as both an expression of personal style and a political statement, at a time when hand-spun cotton still represented the fierce struggle for independence.

Today – seventy-six years on from India's independence – design in India has entered yet another period of change. A new generation, freed from the weight of postcolonial baggage, are bolder in exploring their identity through styles that are shaped according to their own terms. Contemporary design is also fuelled by the open market and a new-found confidence about celebrating Indian craft through a design language infused with references that range broadly from Indian modernism to Mughal royalty and beyond. The sari's dynamism doesn't seem to be merely a passing trend; rather, it seems to be a genuine contemporary movement, shaped by a rapidly shifting culture. Its rejuvenation is being propelled by a new wave of Indian designers who are experimenting with unexpected materials, forms and accessories, including trainers and shirts; popularising pared-back designs; and reintroducing the sari as the height of fashionable contemporary clothing.

I grew up in Britain, the descendent of grandparents who had fled a newly established Pakistan for Bombay – now Mumbai – in the wake of Partition, eventually making their way here in the 1950s. Like most diaspora Indians, I considered the sari to be something worn by my grand-mother or on special occasions such as weddings, though in any case I preferred the lehenga because the sari always seemed difficult to wear: I had the impression the pleats were delicate, their drape and formation harder to achieve and maintain on the body. The sari first caught my attention in a concrete way when I moved to New Delhi in 2015. Saris draped over collared shirts, worn with trainers, belts or blazers by young intellectual women visiting the growing number of contemporary art galleries, or forging a path as writers, looked irresistibly fresh and clean. Generally light and hand-woven, these saris appeared to be free of the burden of ostentation associated with traditional or formal wear. Delving further, I observed designers across Mumbai, Delhi, Kolkata and Bangaluru creating distinctive, wearable saris for younger women; adapting the garment to the urban everyday through playful twists on traditional weaves; employing dyes in a variety of colours, as well as new shapes, patterns and details.

Since then, designers have pushed the boundaries even further. HUEMN's quilted sari, for instance, was designed in parallel with the brand's street-style puffer jackets, introducing a casual urban feel. Playing with form, design studio Bodice incorporates pleats into the structure of sari fabric, taking the pleat beyond the drape to form architectural lines. A distressed denim sari by

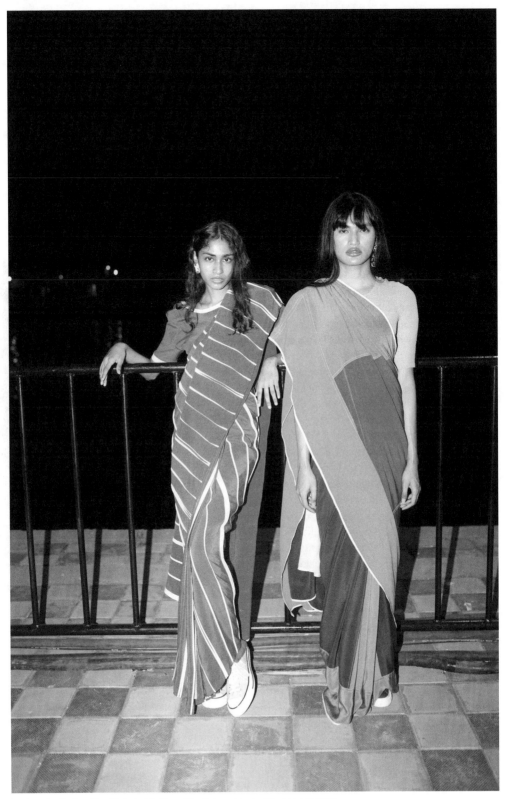

Bodice, the Bodice Rani Pink Sari (left) and the Colour-blocked Sari (right), 2019

Diksha Khanna, styled with a white shirt, applies a ubiquitous material to a totally unexpected context. Then there's the sari beyond the 'sari'. Amit Aggarwal's fascination with materials and complex silhouettes is expressed through pre-stitched sari-like gowns, made from synthetic polymers structured to emulate amoebic forms. Contemporary artist Bharti Kher – making work for the gallery rather than the catwalk – drapes heavily lacquered sari fabric over cast-concrete plinths to create portraits of absent bodies. Each plinth is the approximate weight of the artist, each representing a woman she knows, the drapes becoming an abstract way to reflect the uniqueness of their stories. These sculptures unleash the sari's capacity for abstract representation, capturing the way it can express identity and meaning beyond its literal function as a garment.

Meaning can also be conveyed by the contemporary sari wearer, whose style is itself an act of design. The sari as it is worn today can convey personal, political or playful messages. Like many other forms of clothing, the sari can be accessorised to express individuality, but how it is draped (and by whom) also adds levels of meaning. The sari can be worn to resist the status quo, by turns rejecting conventional notions of womanhood and framing the garment's profound heritage. At the same time, its versatility mobilises a diverse range of progressive voices, personas and agendas. This reclaiming of the sari has involved it becoming a powerful tool for activism in the hands of social-justice groups led by women, such as the Gulabi Gang and the Hargila Army to name just two. Drawing on the legacy of *hijra* or *kinnar* communities, it has also given a voice to those who wish to express their gender fluidity, or to convey messages of body positivity or hybrid national identity. The rise of digital media in India has further enabled the creativity of individual wearers, who are accessorising, draping, mix-and-matching saris and their components to curate a dynamic brand of personal style encapsulated on social media. Hashtags like #sareenotsorry, #sarigram and #sariswap proliferate, transporting this third-century garment into the wardrobes of Gen Z.

Despite the incredible degree of reinvention, certain of the sari's fundamental textile components remain elemental. Its purest form – articulated through its most basic constituent parts: the weave, texture, colour and surface – is still deeply appreciated, even if the mass-produced, power-loom sari holds strong as a commercial product. Continued innovation by craftspeople and designers is pushing the sari's materiality to unknown heights, partly through experimentation with established techniques like *jamdani* and ikat, partly by creating fabrics that are new to the sari, woven from recycled plastics or metal yarn; yet,

Pranjal Gupta, 2021. Sobia Ameen wearing the Arch Sari by Advait with the Padatika Express Shirt by Doh Tak Keh

at the same time, the popularity of more traditional materials like hand-spun, hand-woven cotton – khadi – seems to have come full circle. Designers such as Abraham & Thakore are rethinking the khadi sari's simplicity, in their case through the addition of laminated gold foil, which both upholds and reacts to its traditional form. In this sense, the sari's shapeshifting continues to epitomise the state of Indian identity, striking a fine balance between the nostalgia of tradition and a zest for change.

What does the future hold? A spectrum of views exists. Progressives are unafraid to embrace this fresh vision of the sari wholeheartedly while some conservatives seek to place boundaries on its novelty, attempting to curb its capacity for change or to associate it with a restrictive idea of womanhood. Some claim that the pre-stitched sari is not actually a sari, insisting that in order to constitute a sari the garment must be entirely unstitched, even though pre-stitched saris are embraced by many wearers and designers and are only growing in popularity. Whether the sari will continue to evolve or be tethered to its roots remains to be seen, but if the boundless creativity of designers, wearers and craftspeople is anything to go by, then the spectacular, playful, dynamic sari movement that is already in motion will only continue to flourish. In spite of the political forces of conservatism at play in India today, the fluidity of the sari – and its ability to cut through religious, caste and regional divides – shines through in ways that are at once striking and unique.

1   Bandana Tewari, 'The sari holds our secrets', *Vogue India* (7 March 2022), www.vogue.in/fashion/content/the-sari-holds-our-secrets [Accessed 30 January 2023]

2   CA Bayly, 'The origins of *swadeshi* (home industry): cloth and Indian society 1700–1930', in *The Social Life of Things – Commodities in a Cultural Perspective*, ed. Arjun Appadurai (Cambridge: Cambridge University Press, 1992), 285–321.

3   Skye Thomas, 'The whole nine yards: women reclaiming the sari', *Selvedge,* 77 (2017), 34–36.

4   The *India Today* piece is referred to in Emma Tarlo, *Clothing Matters: Dress and Identity in India* (Chicago, IL: Chicago University Press, 1996), 329.

Cecil Beaton, *Maharani Gayatri Devi*, c.1939–45

SARI
   HEROINES
Throughout history, influential women have worn the sari boldly
and with purpose. Maharani Gayatri Devi's chiffon saris were
fundamental to her persona as a woman of elegance, wealth and status
and became the *de facto* uniform for many royals. Meanwhile, Amrita
Sher-Gil, an early modernist Indian-Hungarian painter, was known for
her bohemian personal style and wore saris as an expression of her
Indian identity, shown through her majestic self-portraits.

André Durst, portrait of *Maharaj Kumar Rani Sita Devi of Kapurthala*, 1934

Raja Ravi Varma, *Portrait of a Lady*, 1893

Amrita Sher-Gil, *Self-Portrait in Blue Sari*, c.1937

THE OFFBEAT SARI

Jamini Roy, *Untitled (Three Women)*, c.1940–50

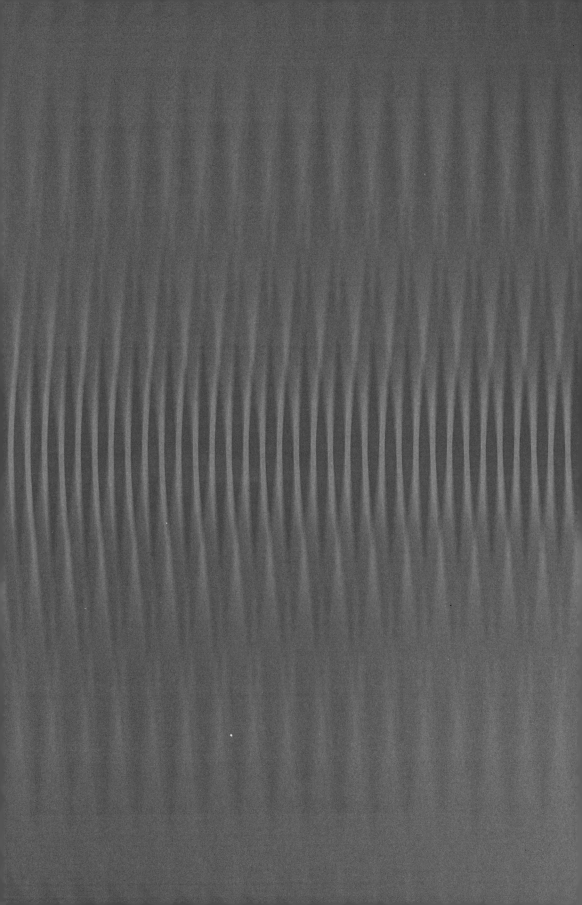

INNOVATION

I

New Aesthetic Fundamentals

Aanchal Malhotra

The founder of AKAARO, Gaurav Jai Gupta, began using
metallic wires of copper and steel in his work as early as
2001, but it was in 2013, while travelling out of Delhi early
one morning, that he chanced upon a coal factory with
plumes of smoke emerging from it. Influenced by that
gritty landscape, alongside his enduring fascination with
the intergalactic, he devised the Liquid Molten Metallic Sari
– first a cool silver, then a luscious gold. When draped, this
sari radiates brilliance, enchanting the eye, yet its shine
is never overpowering.

For Gupta, the sari is a staple; it is India's yesterday,
today and tomorrow. A textile weaver by training, his
strongest relationship is with the loom, which is also
the source for innovation within his oeuvre. As a brand,
AKAARO can be defined as minimalistic, with little embellishment by visible patterns, inspired in part by Japanese
aesthetics. It is a crossover between art and fashion. Its
collection of molten saris, which have quickly become
coveted pieces that influence trends, display a subtlety
and divine quality when draped, a lustre that comes from
the metal used in the weave.

AKAARO, hand-woven Liquid Molten Gold Metallic
Sari, 2016

According to Gupta, the sari as a garment is already
so evolved and finessed, and so embraced by a national
majority, that there is no need per se to redefine its
silhouette. Instead, much of his work has been on the
sari's materiality and tactility. 'When it comes to the sari,
the truly transformative work can happen only in the weave.
It is not about embroidery, perhaps a little about print, but
mostly about the weave – for then you are working around
the core, the structure of the garment,' he says.[1]

The versatility and popularity of the sari derive from the
fact that there was and remains no single way to drape it;
instead, the drape changes according to cultural specifici-
ties, climatic conditions, the formality of the occasion, the

fabric and density of the sari, class and occupation, and its function as a garment. The sari of each region in India has its own style, weave, drape, design, motif, colour and history, handed down through generations. Traditionally, the sari was worn without a blouse on top or a petticoat underneath, until both items were popularised in the late nineteenth century.

On the one hand, the sari has never really evaded our gaze – it remains, quite literally, the uniform of thousands of working women in the country, inescapable in its simplicity. And yet on the other hand, there is a unique disparity between 'the existing chintz of a wedding sari and the almost pallid nature of a daily drape'.[2] Over time, for the modern, urban Indian woman, the sari became largely reserved for special or formal occasions, usually draped with the help of an elder. With the influx of Western fashion, this quintessential Indian classic was tucked beneath the gauze of childhood nostalgia – those memories of watching mothers and grandmothers expertly forming pleat after pleat.

Until the 1990s, though fashion choices on Bollywood screens quickly made their way to the masses with pops of colour and an update to the basic blouse, the appearance of the sari remained largely unchanged.[3] Convention dominated drape and form, tradition eclipsed style, and little work was done to understand how to carry a revered ancient silhouette into a modern world. However, over the past couple of decades, there has been a gradual renewed interest among designers seeking to move the sari beyond its staid form and reimagine it for a younger, urban female wearer, using techniques ranging from embellishments to a total change in the silhouette.

One of the strongest proponents of redefining nostalgic notions to make the traditional sari 'an object of desire for the contemporary, independent and active' woman is Sanjay Garg, creator of the brand Raw Mango.[4] His intervention into traditional hand-loom weaves – particularly Chanderi, which originated in a small town in Madhya Pradesh, and was once used for royal saris and turbans, described as being as light as woven air – has revitalised them into a form that modern women can relate to. Withdrawing from the traditional palette of red, purple, pistachio green, white and black, Raw Mango infuses the sari with a riot of brightness by incorporating shades like ochre yellow, *gulabi* pink, parrot green and lapis blue. These have helped it to gain a new status as everyday wear. Garg is not interested in rejecting tradition altogether, but instead transforms old-world charm into a modern avatar that makes the garment more wearable. Each drape bears evidence of its rich historical lineage. While Garg's collections retain the

Raw Mango, Folia Sari, 2021

THE OFFBEAT SARI

original sari silhouette, he endeavours to create a delicate balance between drawing on the past and looking towards the future.

The first to break the form of the single piece of unstitched fabric was Tarun Tahiliani, who belongs to the first generation of Indian couturiers. His 'concept sari' or 'pre-stitched sari' first hit the runway in 2005/06 as something one could slip into, much like a dress or gown. It was a hassle-free sari, simplified in form yet elaborate in design. With each pleat visibly embracing the female form, this kind of garment was able to explore a number of different drapes and styles – ranging from freer flowing to more structured, worn with corsets, belts and cummerbunds.

Also embracing the sari as a garment to be conceptualised well beyond its most common drape is Rahul Mishra, winner in 2014 of the prestigious International Woolmark Prize in Milan. He often combines stunningly embroidered sheer capes and gauzy jackets with his saris, while retaining traditional Indian motifs and techniques of hand-loom embroidery. Clusters of embellished mushrooms gild the length of the saris, delicate lace flowers function as scalloped borders; indeed, nature is welcomed into nearly every collection. But Mishra's garments, while magnificent, carry a sense of care and critical engagement with the world. He stresses that 'local craft and hand loom continue to be repositories of our ancient heritage' remaking on how 'with suitable design intervention and slight modernisation, these aspects of our lifestyle may gain some relevance for the current consumer'.[5]

The drive towards simpler, sustainable practices, combined with innovation in materials over the last decade, has led to designer Diksha Khanna's patchwork saris. These are made with needlepoint embroidery on hand-loom linens, teamed with scraps of repurposed distressed denim, which lends the garments a youthful rawness. In an interview with *ELLE* magazine, Khanna describes how using denim as a material helps her sari to connect to a younger generation, who 'love this silhouette but are afraid of embracing it due to the manageability factor'.[6]

While designers in the West may try to reinvent older crafts, young Indian designers often begin from the base of artisanship – taking inspiration from their raw materials to express fresh views of modernity and glamour. Rimzim Dadu, whose eponymous brand celebrated its fifteenth anniversary in 2022, designed her first sari nearly ten years into setting up her practice. As someone who had grown up watching her mother wear a crisp sari day after day, she wanted to push the boundaries of what a sari was, which she felt was no less than an 'Indian power-suit'. She describes the sari as something fluid but also very

Diksha Khanna, hand-distressed Denim Sari, 2018

structured, which was the initial concept she wanted to explore. The material she chose was steel – heavy, constraining and yet with the desire to transform it into something drapeable, malleable, soft and airy. Her steel sari, which to Dadu made perfect sense, took nearly eight months of research and development. The final product was an undulating, theatrical, almost sculptural form, polished and reminiscent of an Anish Kapoor artwork or a sweeping Frank Gehry staircase, broadening the concept of the sari while retaining the femininity and fluidity of its traditional silhouette.

A statement (and now cult) piece, Dadu's metal sari consists of hair-thin steel wires woven to form the pallu, and – with the remaining garment being traditional – the full effect is contingent on how the wearer drapes it. Glints appear in the texture, holding within them a magnetic energy as the colours change under different lights. There is a playful youthfulness to the garment, while still exuding confidence – a fine balance to maintain. For Dadu, clothes 'are neither costume nor embellishment' but an homage to raw materials. She enjoys creating a sculptural unexpectedness in her work, and from the colours she chooses – midnight blues, vibrant pinks, golden yellows – to her textured forms, there is a clear intention to dress the modern Indian woman.

In the essay 'Conversations with Contemporary India', Maria Elettra Verrone and Massimo Warglien describe how true stylistic innovations come from the human imagination: 'Rethinking female fashion means conceiving a new female body, outside the family places and ritual occasions, to express itself at work, in urban social life and in experimenting with new ways of showing and expressing oneself.'[7] With the fashion brand HUEMN, a wordplay on 'hue' and 'human', co-founder and Creative Director Pranav Kirti Misra has attempted to redefine perceptions of the body and of the garment that adorns it. While there may be only a few saris in HUEMN's body of work (though the brand celebrated its tenth anniversary in 2022), there is certainly no dearth of innovation. Misra states that with 'the overlapping roles of women today, and the limitation of time, the sari has become an impractical garment and requires the ease of wearability, rather than just the ease of concept'.[8] He argues that, while garments like trousers and skirts have changed over the years, the sari has been very little influenced by the West. He wonders whether this is the reason why major changes to the garment have been mostly at the surface level, with embellishments or accessories. 'There is a nostalgia attached to the sari, an emotional history, which is why we love [it], but it is equally important for it to find some kind of global relevance and be made practical for the global woman today.'[9]

HUEMN, Hybrid Sari-Pants, 2022

It is from this conceptual framework that the Quilted Sari emerged. In 2015, while creating a collection of outerwear inspired by jackets and quilts, Misra reflected on the climatic restraints of a sari, wondering why it couldn't be a complete garment in its own right – able to adjust to the temperature outside. In response, he devised a fully quilted pallu, which could be wrapped around the wearer almost like a windcheater. More recently, Misra toyed with the idea of a sari being a symmetrical garment with a pallu on both shoulders, which is how the nuanced Hybrid Sari-Pants came into being. Seen from a distance, the garment comprises a pre-stitched sari-pant with a high neckline, a very slight hint of naked waist and fabric draped to the floor, worn with seamless opera gloves – appearing less like a sari and more like a dress with a cape. Viewed up close, however, its intended effect differs depending on how it is styled and carried. Because there is very little to distract the eye by way of exposed skin, you can admire the beauty of the overlapping pallus and the effortlessly diaphanous silk. Even while being the least sari-forward sari, it manages to create the aura of a feminine silhouette. Misra dubs it a 'sari which can be worn in fifty-seven seconds'. At one level, it is a dress; at another, due to the fact that it has two legs, it is also a pair of trousers; and, of course, it is a sari. It is thus a fusion of different garments from different parts of the world, a collaboration between various sensitivities.

Thousands of years since its inception, the sari remains indispensable to Indian culture – held close to the hearts and histories of many. It is an emotive garment of memory and myth, of storytelling and image-building. It is an endur-ing garment of our mothers and grandmothers, but also of workers and politicians and teachers as well as of haute couture and royalty. One of the greatest strengths of the sari is that it collaborates in its own modernisation. For the Indian designer today, the venerable sari evokes far more than mere sartorial and functional history – it champions inclusivity and, whether in its conventional form or subject to evolution and reimagination, it has over the centuries become generous enough to embrace within its folds multiple iterations, generations and aesthetic choices.

1   From a telephone interview conducted with Gupta in December 2022.

2   Tanya Mehta, 'Sari Stories: The Art of Revival', *Grazia* (30 April 2019).

3   Roshni Verma, 'Tracing the Evolution of Sarees', *Pernia's Pop-up Blog* (14 February 2020), blog.perniaspop-upshop.com/evolution-of-saree [Accessed 8 February 2023]

4   Maria Elettra Verrone and Massimo Warglien, 'Conversations with Contemporary India', in *There's Something in the Air: Life Stories from Italy and India*, ed. Lorenzo Angeloni and Maria Elettra Verrone (New Delhi: Juggernaut Publishers, 2018), 327.

5   Deepali Nandwani, 'Exclusive: Rahul Mishra, Anavila Misra and Priyanka Modi on Indian fashion's big challenges – digital retail and transformed consumer', *Moneycontrol* (22 August 2020), www.moneycontrol.com/news/trends/features/exclusive-rahul-mishra-anavila-misra-and-priyanka-modi-on-indian-fashions-big-challenges-digital-retail-and-transformed-consumer-5738541.html [Accessed 2 February 2023]

6   'Fresh fashion label to know: Diksha Khanna', *ELLE*, www.elle.in/article/fashion-designer-diksha-khanna-sonam-kapoor-denim-sari [Accessed 3 February 2023]

7   Verrone and Warglien, 327.

8   From a telephone interview conducted with Misra in December 2022.

9   Ibid.

Sabyasachi Mukherjee

Interviewed by Priya Khanchandani

Sabyasachi Mukherjee has established one of the most influential luxury fashion businesses of recent decades by bringing craft heritage to a contemporary bridal client-base. Having graduated from Kolkata's National Institute of Fashion Technology in 1999, Mukherjee began his eponymous label with a studio consisting of three workers. Since then, the international appeal of his label has led to showcases at all the major fashion weeks – including New York, Paris and Milan – as well as winning Best Costume Design at the 2005 National Film Awards for Sanjay Leela Bhansali's feature film *Black*. Mukherjee also brought Indian couture to Christian Louboutin, when they collaborated on a collection of shoes in 2017.

Based in Kolkata, he makes clothes with strong connections to the city's heritage, drawing inspiration from Bengali culture through embellishments such as patchwork, *bandhani* tie-dye and *gota* embroidery. These craft processes, brought together as the signature style of his cult bridal collections, have seen Sabyasachi create wedding dresses for Bollywood celebrities like Deepika Padukone and Priyanka Chopra. Mukherjee discusses his ongoing commitment to championing the sari with the Design Museum's Head of Curatorial, and curator of *The Offbeat Sari* exhibition, Priya Khanchandani.

RIGHT   Umrao Singh Sher-Gil. Amrita Sher-Gil
         wearing a zari sari, Simla, India c.1936
OVERLEAF Natasha Poonawalla wearing a bustier
         by Daniel Roseberry for Schiaparelli
         with custom couture sari and train by
         Sabyasachi, 2022; Sabyasachi Mukherjee,
         Yellow Floral Sari, 2018

PRIYA KHANCHANDANI   Do you think craft is valued enough in India now?

SABYASACHI MUKHERJEE
It's sometimes hard when you have proximity, because it's a human tendency not to value things that are close to you. It was put very beautifully by Rabindranath Tagore. He wrote that he travelled the world looking for beauty, visited different countries, climbed hills and valleys, glided over oceans, just to come back and realise that beauty lay on a dewdrop on a blade of grass, right on his doorstep.[1]

It sums up India's attitude towards craft: because we have so much of it, we haven't been able to give it the respect it truly deserves. But in the last ten to fifteen years, the Indian fashion industry has developed a design culture that is deeply invested in craft – not just myself, but also designers like Ritu Kumar, Anamika Khanna, Raw Mango and many others. Respect for craft has grown more and more.

PK   Back in 2013, you initiated the 'Save the Sari' project, which is a non-profit initiative to support regional weaves by artisans. What were your motivations for doing so, and how you did you go about it?

SM   I work with a lot of weavers, and this was something that I did at a time when I could not give enough work to my weavers. A lot of them were making very high-end products for me, but the lower end of the market was where they made their money. I decided to work with a few clusters of weavers from India. I would buy

their saris at their prices and put my stamp of curation on them. Then we would sell the garments out of my stores without turning a profit, only marking them up for overheads and back-end costs. The idea was to be able to put these everyday weaves in proximity to a design brand, which gave them a much-needed elevated status. We did that for a few years until we were able to give enough work to our weavers, so that they didn't have to look for work elsewhere.

PK   Are saris your most popular garment in terms of sales? Or is it the lehenga?

SM   You know, the sari is the fastest growing category in my business, and it's becoming more and more universal. Until about five or six years ago, when I was doing a lot of celebrity weddings, people were still buying Sabyasachi lehengas. Now a lot of modern women are choosing to wear a sari for a wedding over a lehenga because they think it's more sustainable, there's less wastage. People want to spend money in the right way and not do

so mindlessly. When you wear a lehenga, you don't wear it more than once or twice, whereas a sari can be worn again and again.

PK   I wondered if you could expand on the definition of the sari, which you've referred to in the past as an important aspect of Indian national identity.[2] What does the sari mean to you? And why do you feel it's so intrinsic to the identity of India?

SM   I was born in 1974 in Bengal and all I saw around me were women wearing saris. My mother went to art school, so she knew a lot of very empowered bohemian women, and I was fascinated by how the sari seemed to adapt itself to every personality. It's a very passive garment: how you choose to wear a sari becomes the sari. A sari can be dignified, it can be powerful, it can be demure, it can be sexy, it can be modern – all depending on how you wear and style it. That is one of the reasons I like the sari: its versatility.

Second, in a sea of cotton-stitched and tailored garments, the sari is ultra-modern in its simplicity. Yet at the same time, because it's an ancient textile, it retains a very organic, spiritual quality that is strangely timeless. When I look at visuals of India, whether pre-independence or post-independence, some of the greatest leaders of the country – poets, artists, actors, politicians, businesswomen – have all worn saris, whether it's [Bollywood actor] Rekha or [modern artist] Amrita Sher-Gil.

PK   We've talked a little about the growing popularity of the sari. The implication of that, of course, is that there was a time when it was waning in popularity, which probably coincided with you growing up. Could you reflect on why the sari experienced that period of decline?

SM   I think there were very concrete social, political and economic reasons why the sari became unpopular. A lot of it has to do with patriarchy. I think a lot of women in India were forced by their families to wear a sari, and a lot of women stopped wearing the sari as an act of silent rebellion. But eventually people always come back to their roots. Today, if you look at emancipated Indian women with a global education, women who have always had freedom of choice, they often choose to wear the sari. I think the reason the sari has returned is because the freedoms that women in this part of the world have enjoyed over the last few decades have been very different from those their mothers and grandmothers may have experienced.

PK   You've talked previously about minimalism as a force that perhaps doesn't belong in India. I wondered if your view on that had shifted at all with the growing popularity of lighter, less embellished saris?

SM   I am all for minimalism, and I'm all for maximalism! I just like the sari to be in its purest form. Whether you're wearing a Kanjeevaram or a khadi sari, I'm all for it. Personally, I think that India shifts effortlessly between minimalism and maximalism. Sometimes a woman will wear

a Banarasi sari with a lot of jewellery, so it'll be 'more is more'; sometimes she'll wear spectacular accessories with something very simple, which is a combination of minimalism and maximalism. But even the simplest of saris is still maximal- ist in terms of craft. It takes time to weave – it's not something that just emerges from a machine. I also like the whole ceremony that goes into wearing a sari.

PK   Let's turn back to maxi- malism to talk about the three

Sabyasachi saris we're showing in the exhibition. The first of these was worn by Natasha Poonawalla in the first ever appearance of a sari at the Met Gala. It was an extremely bold statement, this Renaissance-esque figure pairing the sari with a Schiaparelli bustier. Could you tell me about the technique involved in making that sari, and what it signified for you to see it represented in that context?

SM   It was Natasha's idea to wear a sari with a Schiaparelli

bustier. I was very amused, and not entirely convinced in the beginning. But Natasha being Natasha, I knew that she would pull it off. What excited me the most was the fact that we were celebrating the Gilded Age. When you think of the Gilded Age, you think of excess and, although it's a cliché, I wanted to create a modern, progressive version of the maharani [queen]. Whenever people think of India, they tend to think of decadence – of gilded palaces, of kings and queens and their jewels and all the exuber- ance of their lives. It's playing into a slightly Orientalist trope imported from the West, but it's also a form of fantasy.

We went for a tulle sari, which was hand-printed and completely studded with stones, pearls and jewels. I wanted to find a way to make the sari a little 'magpie'. We had these tiny velvet pits that almost looked like ostrich eggs – they were stitched on to the fabric by hand, which made it almost like a 'curiosity' sari. It was both very, very excessive, yet very modern at the same time. The whole thing came together with the hair, the make-up, the jewel- lery and the Schiaparelli bustier.

PK   We're also showing the Bengal Tiger Couture Sari worn by Deepika Padukone at Cannes, which is made of chiffon and crêpe with block-print stripes and embellished with crystals and sequins. What was your vision for that sari?

SM   Deepika rang me up and we agreed she should wear a sari. I was fascinated at that time with Brigitte Bardot and Amy Winehouse, and I envisaged something that was both modern and rock 'n' roll. I was thinking of all the 1970s clothing, which had these bold, flat stripes. I knew I wanted to do something that was Indian, and very modern, but also something a little bit retro in a way that was easily identifiable. So I said, 'Let's make a sari with the stripes of the Bengal tiger', which is also my brand's signature. We gave it an evening look by overlaying the print with sequins, and then Deepika did the cat-eye makeup with a messy bouffant. There was a certain volatile sexuality and naughtiness – it was very cosmopolitan.

PK   The third sari of yours we're showing is the Yellow Floral Sari with the blouse and belt. I wanted to ask about your interest in floral prints, which has been responsible for a resurgence in the popularity of chintzes in Indian fashion. Where did your fascination for those kinds of patterns arise from, and why do you think they've become so trendy?

SM   I think my aesthetic appreciation for florals derives from three things: British pubs, British bed and breakfasts, and *The Sound of Music*. I come from Kolkata, which was the British capital in India at one point. Kolkata has a lot of quaint hotels that look just like British bed and breakfasts or pubs. So you have this aesthetic that I love, which is just print on print – where they take one print and turn it into curtains, cushions, drapes, blankets, quilts. That was my fascination with *The Sound of Music* – the scene where Maria takes curtains and makes clothes for all the children! And, of course, my hyper-saturated colours and

my precision with tropical flowers come from Frida Kahlo's aesthetic, and how she used to weave flowers into her braids. One of the reasons I love doing floral prints is because they are accessible to women who can't always buy couture. I think sometimes you can create maximalism using maximalist prints, without burning a hole in people's pockets.

1   Quotation paraphrased from Rabindranath Tagore's signed note to the film director Satyajit Ray, 1928.
2   See Border&Fall, 'Sari Symbolism: with Sabyasachi', www.borderand-fall.com/sabyasachi-mukherjee-sari [Accessed 26 January 2023]

ABOVE   Munsif Molu, 2019. Elizabeth Mech Boro wearing hand-woven molten
             chevron blue, aqua green and gold metallic saris by AKAARO
RIGHT   Aakanksha Arun, 2019. Gautami Reddy wearing Liquid Molten
             Textured Sari by AKAARO

AKAARO, Colour palette selection for the Temple Run Sari, inspired by the architecture of Kanchipuram, 2022

AKAARO, Temple Run Sari, 2022

THE OFFBEAT SARI

Manou, 2016. Pallavi Singh wearing hand-woven Caramel Liquid Molten Metallic Sari by AKAARO

ABOVE + BELOW   Bodice, making of the Bodice Sari, 2018
LEFT   Bodice, the Bodice Multi-binding Sari, 2021

ASHDEEN, China Town Sari, Chinoi-sari collection, 2017

ASHDEEN

The intricate China Town Sari is the result of centuries of cross-cultural exchange between China and India. The sari's design revives a style called Parsi Gara – adopted by the Parsi community, who migrated to India from Persia and were influenced by the embroidery they brought back from China during the opium trade under colonial rule. Designer Ashdeen Z Lilaowala adds contemporary twists, such as the deep aubergine colour. Scaled-up Chinese–Indian motifs demonstrate the surprising impact of globalisation on the sari's rich history.

A group of Parsi women dressed in traditional garas, date unknown

ASHDEEN, detail of China Town Sari, Chinoi-sari collection, 2017

HUEMN, back view of Quilted Sari, 2017

HUEMN, Quilted Sari, 2017

HUEMN, Hybrid Sari-Pants, 2022

ABOVE   NORBLACK NORWHITE, Shimma Sari, 2017
LEFT + OVERLEAF   NORBLACK NORWHITE, making of the
Shimma Sari, 2017

Raw Mango, Bodhi Sari, Monkey Business collection, 2016

Raw Mango, Ensal Sari, Other collection, 2021

Raw Mango, Guler Sari, Angoori collection, 2019

Raw Mango, Siori Sari, Other collection, 2021

ABOVE   Raw Mango, Sanzen Sari, Monkey Business collection, 2016
RIGHT   Raw Mango, Azaana Sari, Sher Bagh collection, 2021

SABYASACHI
× SCHIAPARELLI

This showstopping ensemble juxtaposes a flowing gold sari by
Sabyasachi with the armour of a gold Schiaparelli bustier. Worn by
Indian businesswoman Natasha Poonawalla at the 2022 Met Gala,
it was the first time a sari had ever been worn at this celebrated
New York event. The embroidered tulle sari with a dramatic train
was paired with the bodice by stylist Anaita Shroff Adajania in
a radical interpretation of the dress code, 'Gilded Glamour'.

THIS SPREAD   Greg Swales, 2022. Natasha Poonawalla wearing bustier by Schiaparelli, with custom couture sari
and train by Sabyasachi Mukherjee for the 2022 Met Gala, *In America: An Anthology of Fashion*

FORM

Fluid Architectures

Anupama Kundoo and Priya Khanchandani

Embedded in the architecture of the sari is a multi-layered story, gathered over time. Throughout its history, the sari has known many guises – its diversity finding expression through variations in textile, weave and in many other aspects. Its fluidity is exemplified in its varied drapes, which determine how the sari takes its form. Traditionally, the only non-negotiable element of the sari was a single, orthogonal length of fabric, typically six yards long (5.5 metres). A sari can, however, be as long as nine yards (8.2 metres) in regions where it is worn draped between the legs. Accompanying it is generally a blouse, and a waistband or petticoat that serves as a 'line' into which the sari's skirt can be tucked. But none of these elements is a given for the contemporary sari, whose mutability leaves it open to seemingly boundless modes of reinvention and new forms of accessory.

From an architect's perspective, the sari could be read as a structure that hinges on three key elements: the border; the body; and the pallu, which hangs over the shoulder. The construction of the border is typically more elaborate than the other elements, with the top edge tucked into the petticoat and the bottom edge touching the feet. This border is often stiffened with a 'fall', an additional band of fabric that is stitched on the inside – enhancing the flow of the drape and protecting the border from wear and tear as it grazes along the floor. The border and the pallu provide a rich canvas for the expression of complex craft techniques, while the freely hanging pallu – the most visible element in the majority of sari drapes – offers a grand climax.

Unlike the rigid structure of a building, the sari's architecture is fluid and easily adapted. Depending on the preferred length of the pallu, the pleats can absorb endless (re)adjustment to accommodate, for example, changes to a woman's body through pregnancy. The pleats can be broad and few or narrow and numerous, but generally have a uniform width determined by a handspan. They are shaped by methodically folding the fabric around the index and little finger, a process that is repeated multiple times to form a bunch of drapes that are then tucked in to prevent them falling into disarray. The most widespread form of pleat, for what is known as the Nivi drape, involves a one-directional, anti-clockwise wrap, with the pleats gathered near the belly button and the loose end of the sari hung over the left shoulder.

Styles of sari drape diverge a great deal across South Asia, from Kodagu to Bengal and further east, and include three-piece saris that comprise a blouse, draped skirt and shawl, as traditionally found in Kerala. In Tamil Nadu, there is a half-sari for young girls who are growing into the sari and still adjusting to the drape. This consists of a wide skirt, a blouse and a separate cloth that is tucked into the skirt then draped across the front diagonally and over the shoulder. The contemporary designs sold by the likes of Utsav Fashion and Lashkaraa reflect these traditions in half-and-half saris that combine two separate fabrics, either matching or contrasting. These have also led to the creation of pre-pleated, ready-to-wear half-and-half saris that save the wearer the effort of draping, and are offered by retailers such as Kalki Fashion. These examples show how the sari has become a language, expressed through fabric, that is indicative of local tastes, environment, function and craft heritage.

Multiple iterations of the sari's drape, however, have fallen out of frequent use, by and large superseded in recent years by the surging popularity of the Nivi form. In an effort to reinstate the heterogeneity of sari drapes and to grow awareness of how to achieve more wearability through a plethora of regional alternatives, creative agency Border&Fall commissioned a series of digital films depicting eight sari drapes that have already been substantially documented in ethnographic research and scholarly literature, but have never been readily accessible online. Advised by Ṛta Kapur Chishti, author of *Saris of India: Tradition and Beyond*, the project draws on extensive cultural fieldwork to present a publicly available inventory of drapes to a curious audience. Interestingly, the intention here was not necessarily to restore the sari's lost heritage but rather to promote its relevance today by recording its varied forms, thereby asserting its contemporaneity rather than clinging to its past.[1] As the founder of Border&Fall, Malika Kashyap, proposes, 'Let's say we tied the pallu like a belt, do away with pleats to create a ghaghra-like skirt with the fabric, wear the sari like a dhoti with a knot at the waist instead of a petticoat. Will these historically available options essentially make the sari more functional as a contemporary garment?'[2]

Border&Fall, *The Sari Series*, 2017. Yakshagana Kase Drape, Karnataka, sari courtesy of Leela Kalyanaraman

In formal terms, the contemporary sari seems to know no limits. Emerging designers are re-creating the sari in ways that challenge its architecture by doing away with border, body and pallu as distinct elements altogether. The main body may be decorated or woven in a single pattern; there may be different, often elaborate, pallus at either end of the fabric, so that the wearer can choose which end to expose, offering myriad options as to how to drape it. Moreover, there may be saris with two entirely different borders, often woven in contrasting colours – such as the Ganga-Jamuna Border saris by Nalli, a heritage brand based in Tamil Nadu. This style enables the wearer to 'swap' or invert the top and bottom (or the beginning and end) of the fabric while draping it, achieving two completely distinct colour combinations with the same piece of textile. Elsewhere, the reversible silk sari by contemporary designer Payal Khand-wala, hand-woven in West Bengal, unleashes the inherent versatility of an unstitched garment by allowing the wearer to 'flip' the sari.

Meanwhile, contemporary designers are working with a living tradition of new sari forms, among them established couturiers like Satya Paul and Anamika Khanna but also smaller studios. Naushad Ali, an emerging designer from Puducherry in Tamil Nadu, designed multiple collections of stitched garments inspired by the sari, but, more recently, he has returned to designing the sari itself – both under his own label and for numerous other sari brands. The globalised culture of the nearby town of Auroville has had a significant influence on his work, leading him to create saris using Indian textiles but combined with blouses influenced by Western dress. Growing up, his interest lay in textile design since his father owned a fabric shop, then later evolved into a desire to study design at the National Institute of Fashion Technology in Chennai. Ali now enjoys making his own textiles, working within the constraints of and exploring the opportunities offered by the hand loom.

Payal Khandwala, Champagne Sari, 2023

One of Ali's pre-stitched sari dresses incorporates a single sleeve, stitched into the body, to hold the sari firmly in place on the shoulder. The wearer must put the sleeve on first then reverse drape the pleats, features which bring just the slightest touch of formality because they emulate the experience of putting on a blazer. As part of his process, Ali had deliberately listed all the elements that define a sari, foregrounding the grace it conveys, to produce a playful collection based around the intersections of these multifarious elements. Sometimes he included the pleat and not the pallu, elsewhere he incorporated the pallu and not the pleat, offering the wearer an opportunity to enjoy individual elements of the sari without having to opt for the whole garment. In fashionable circles today, people may not know

Naushad Ali, hand-woven sari with a stitched jacket sleeve on the pallu, 2017

Naushad Ali, natural indigo-dyed sari with upcycled yarns and hand-crocheted blouse, 2019

THE OFFBEAT SARI

how to wear a sari or feel comfortable carrying it off, but – through these new approaches to the drape – are still able enjoy the sensation of wearing one.

Even amid the prevalence of ready-made garments, the sari remains valued and honoured in South Asia – unlike in other regions, where local dress has been more comprehensively superseded by Western dress. Its materiality has been conducive to its longevity. To create a handmade sari requires immense skill and time, so it can be expensive. And yet, being both long-lasting and unrestricted by the limitations of sizing, they are often handed down from generation to generation, forming a circular economy of saris that enables them to outlive the disenchantments of any individual wearer. In this context, the sari remains a deeply sentimental garment, and one that offers a rebuke to the fickle affective investments of fast fashion.

In whichever form it comes, the sari continues to be a powerful symbol of intergenerational identity, retaining its association with honour and elegance. Progressive young designers, like Naushad Ali, are engaged in creating fresh clothing for a global clientele, yet find themselves unable to detach their new work from the sari – mesmerised by its classic appeal. For Ali, the enduring values of the sari transcend the brief shelf-life of passing trends and it remains an endless wellspring of new ideas: 'It is like a gold mine for me to play with. That's it!'

1   See Ṛta Kapur Chishti and Martand Singh, *Saris of India: Tradition and Beyond* (New Delhi: Roli Books, 2013).
2   Shefalee Vasudev, 'Our many sari selves', *Mint* (8 November 2016), www.livemint.com/Leisure/qFxjp954Y2qKclo1uid2DI/Our-many-sari-selves.html [Accessed 3 February 2023]

Amit

Aggarwal

Interviewed by Phyllida Jay

Amit Aggarwal is a fashion designer who brings the glamour of couture to the clothes he creates through what he describes as 'the engineering of organic forms'. This term refers to his use of structural fabrics influenced by exoskeletons or cocoon shapes found in nature. Drawing on encounters with the arts and sciences in his early childhood, his pre-stitched saris and gowns often employ recycled materials such as repurposed vintage fabric and industrial waste, as well as making experimental use of unusual materials such as polymers. Aggarwal began his career as an assistant designer for couturier Tarun Tahiliani, having graduated from New Delhi's National Institute of Fashion Technology in 1999 and worked extensively in Europe and Japan.

Since the launch of his own label in 2012, Aggarwal's commercial success has seen him speak at TED India on the future of fashion, exhibit at the ARKEN Museum near Copenhagen and show at numerous Paris Fashion Weeks. In 2021, he opened an experiential Mumbai flagship store inspired by the sea and the winds of the city. He is interviewed here by Phyllida Jay, an anthropologist specialising in contemporary Indian fashion and craft culture. Their discussion covers the isolation of lockdown, taking pleasure in the everyday and how Aggarwal's creativity is guided by organic life forms and biomimicry.

RIGHT   Amit Aggarwal with a *kaarigar* (artisan) working
on the Metanoia Sari, 2023
OVERLEAF   Amit Aggarwal, hand-embroidered leaf cape,
The Metanoia collection, 2021

PHYLLIDA JAY You've described your approach as 'the engineering of organic forms'.[1] Why do the unbounded and wild forces of the natural world, in particular the sea and aquatic life forms, hold such a fascination for you as a designer?

AMIT AGGARWAL It has to do with my early years. My father is an engineer, and he does a lot of architectural drawings, while my mother had always dreamt of being a doctor and had a great personal love for and interest in biology. A very simple example is that my mother would always wear a red flower in her hair throughout my childhood. That is why, I think, I drew my first inspirations from the natural world. My father influenced me to see how everything in the natural world has an architectural structure: the ability to give formal expression to its own life force. There's an interaction between organic life and the form through which that life is best able to sustain itself. I suspect that's what led to my love for biomimicry.

PJ The Metanoia Sari has a very beautiful undulating drape and form. Can you talk a bit about the inspiration for this piece?

AA The sari was designed during the peak of the first wave of the pandemic. I found a lot of solace in three things – which kept me alive at that point, because I was all by myself. I hadn't seen my boyfriend for almost five months: it was the longest we had gone without seeing each other. I took comfort in nature. Every day I spent time on my balcony, just enjoying the three life forms:

air, water and earth. That slowly became the basis of the entire collection.

The sari brings together three elements in one piece. The bodice looks like a coral reef underwater. Then the drape, or the bottom part of it, is a hand-marbled textile, which resonates with the many layers of terrain beneath the Earth. The pallu is designed to look like air when it moves over the surface of sand or water, and it evokes air circling around the body – transparent, fluid and light. These

three elements came together to form the piece, a work in progress that arose out of the feeling of closely observing nature.

PJ Generally, when we think about the sari drape, we think about it in terms of the fabric. But you've just described the drape of the Metanoia Sari in terms of air. Can you describe the process of conceptualising and creating that with your unique approach to materials?

AA This particular piece synthesises three different methods

of what we imagine or what we define to be craftsmanship, at least in relation to India. There is the traditional craftsmanship of beading, of hand embroidery, which you can easily see: the body of the sari is completely constructed out of beading.

I feel that the country is also known for its incredible printing techniques, which have an alchemical relationship to materials that goes beyond embellishment. So that's why there is a marbled surface that replicates the geological layers of the Earth.

It also raises the question, 'Where does the future of craftsmanship lie?' Does it always need to be based around tradition? Or can we mix the traditional with science or technology to create a new language of design? The plissé pallu is basically first completely created by hand. Then it goes under a heat-setting machine to pleat it, interweaving handcraft with machine technology.

If you hold one of our pieces, it doesn't weigh more than a kilo. So that's one of the more significant talking points: women enjoy the sari's lightness. That is one of its core qualities: despite looking like metal, which makes it appear extremely strong, it's actually very light and moves with the wind.

PJ You have a unique approach to textile development and making, often using upcycled and unconventional materials like polymers. Can you talk about the origins and challenges of this approach? How does this making process work in crafting the drapes and folds of the sari? Obviously, when we talk about the sari in India, we often talk about

THE OFFBEAT SARI

the hand-loom textile, and the ideology behind that. But you do something quite different. What is your vision and philosophy?

AA   It emerges from the environment I grew up in, where things weren't immediately discarded. We would actually reuse them for multiple purposes. I feel that somehow, when I started looking at materials for my collections, the attraction to recycled or unconventional materials wasn't part of a very conscious thought process – it was just what I knew.

When I was looking for a space to start a small unit, I was passing by a factory in Okhla [a village near the border between Delhi and Uttar Pradesh], and I found scraps of polymer which caught my attention. When I started the company, I didn't have a lot of resources – barely enough money to buy a cutting table and two machines. In India, we have a word, *jugaad*, which basically translates as 'necessity is the mother of invention'. I started looking at leftover fabrics and scraps. India is a huge textile- and fashion-producing country, so there are a lot of markets that are dumps of really wonderful surplus and waste fabric. Because I didn't have enough money to go and buy luxurious fabrics from Italy, for the first few collections I would buy leftover fabric from a lot of these markets. Somehow that developed into a unique language.

I wouldn't say that this was a conscious marketing decision ... that I wanted to 'go out and save the world'. It's rather that the biggest lesson my parents gave me was to live a life consciously, where I appreciate the small day-to-day things.

PJ   I find the biomimicry that informs your work fascinating. You have the fluid, soft, unstructured fabric or drape. But then you also have this structure that you create using polymers, which almost forms a carapace. You're doing this at an incredible, couture-level of artisanal process. How have you developed this approach?

AA   What I understand of biomimicry is that a certain thing lasts or exists because it's been able to adapt. That's why life continues to sustain multiple forms. You can look at a material, break it down and restructure it to give it a newer language. That is what excites me about a material: the fact that we can change its forms with the introduction of other materials. I enjoy how this can lead to multiple possibilities.

The one crucial thing is that, incidentally, many pieces that the studio makes might start with a very distinct idea of what the final piece needs to be or should look like. The Metanoia Sari was a process; I don't think I imagined it or sketched it out right at the beginning. It was more of a collage, where different textiles came together and sat with each other effortlessly to create this piece. It's more something that happened out of different things speaking to each other and forming an alliance.

I've always been inspired by the Brutalist structures of Zaha Hadid. The way she experimented with form and scale was staggering. It allows you to understand the possibilities of couture, too: the spectacle and the formlessness of it.

Form in my work depicts the weightlessness of the ocean, the caress of the wind and the cradle of the Earth as they nurture you. We've been strongly inspired by the beauty of nature. Sea foam, deep forest green and sky blue are the main colours utilised in our collections. In 2020, we created a three-dimensional winged lehenga inspired by the fins of a fish reimagined as wings. In this sari for the exhibition, we have been inspired by the ethereal lightness of the Earth, the many textures in its cracked field and everything in between.

1   Phyllida Jay, *Fashion India* (London: Thames & Hudson, 2015), 199.

Amit Aggarwal, the Metanoia Sari, the Metanoia collection, 2021

Amit Aggarwal, hand-woven structured gown, the
Metanoia collection, 2021

Kallol Datta, Look 11, Volume 1, 2018

Kallol Datta, Look 5, Volume 1, 2018

Naushad Ali, hand-woven mulberry silk sari and blouse, 2020

THE OFFBEAT SARI

Kallol Datta, Object 13, Volume 2, 2019

Raghubir Singh, *Monsoon Rains, Monghyr, Bihar*, 1967

THE OFFBEAT SARI

Bharti Kher, detail of *Portrait: Manju*, 2013

Bharti Kher, *Portrait: Manju*, 2013

BHARTI KHER

Heavily lacquered saris, draped on cast-concrete plinths, create portraits of absent bodies in this series of sculptures by Bharti Kher. The sari recalls the artist's childhood: her father worked in textiles and her mother was a dressmaker in a fabric shop. Here, the sari is abstracted to the point where it becomes a substance – in the artist's words, 'almost like pigment, like paint'.

ABOVE + BELOW   Studio Medium, Hands-free Sari, 2022
RIGHT   Studio Medium, wrapped Polka Itajime saris, 2022

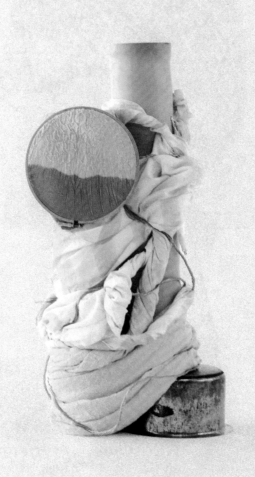

Border&Fall, *The Sari Series*, 2017.
Boggili Posi Kattukodam Drape,
Andhra Pradesh, sari by Taanbaan

ABOVE   Border&Fall, *The Sari Series*, 2017. Kotapad Drape,
Orissa, sari courtesy of Anita Lal
LEFT   Border&Fall, *The Sari Series*, 2017. Ranchi Saiko
Drape, Jharkhand, sari by Swati & Sunaina

THE SARI
SERIES

The Sari Series is an online anthology that documents more than
eighty sari drapes from across India. Shifting the focus away from
textile design, these short 'how to drape' films are intended to encour-
age experimentation with sari silhouettes. The popular drapes pictured
here – the Boggili Posi Kattukodam, Ranchi Saiko and Kotapad – show
varying degrees of complexity.

ABOVE   Naushad Ali, hand-woven silk-cotton sari, 2020
RIGHT   Naushad Ali, recycled fabric waste woven as a sari and overdyed
             in natural indigo, 2019
OVERLEAF   Irene Yee, *Embracing All: Prerna Dangi*, 2022. Sari by Satya Paul

Rashmi Varma, 2×1 Sari, 2017

THE OFFBEAT SARI

Payal Khandwala, Jamdani collection, 2022

THIS SPREAD   Payal Khandwala, Gemini collection, 2018

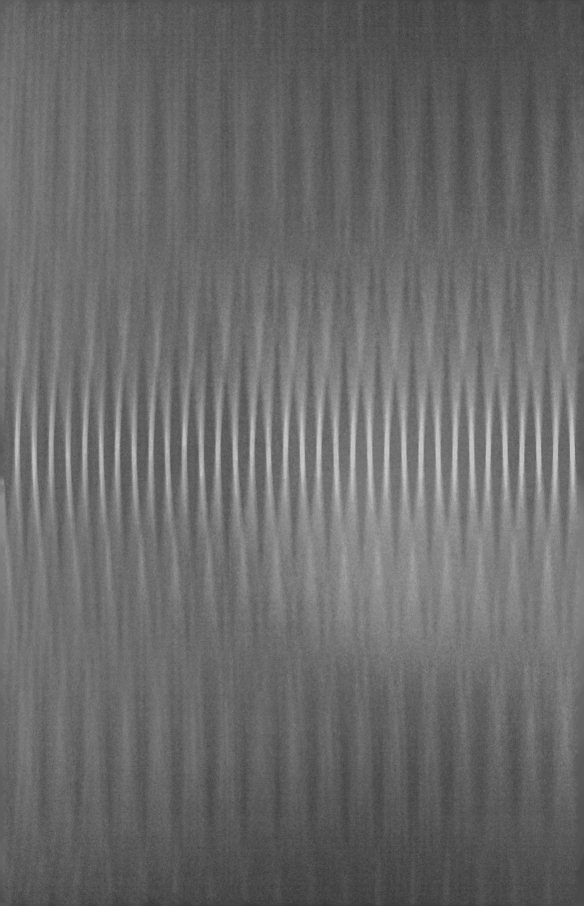

IDENTITY

Ways of Embodying

Pragya Agarwal

I was fourteen years old when I wore a sari for the first
time. It signified stepping into womanhood, coming of age.
It was a symbol of femininity. I had never felt the desire to
wear a sari before then, always seeing it as trapping: nine
yards of fabric binding women into a life of subservience.
I had seen my mother and other women of her generation
wear a sari all the time, every day. I had decided that I
didn't want a life like theirs. I had also seen the women in
saris in Bollywood. Here, the sari was sexy and modest at
the same time, the pallu on the head a sign of respect and
humility, the jewelled cholis with the pallu tucked in the
waist were sensual and seductive. The sari was both regal
and run-of-the-mill, but almost always a symbol of femininity – deployed in strategic ways for either covering or
enhancing a woman's body. I had read no feminist literature,
nor learned the word 'feminist', yet unknowingly I was one.
And, in resisting the gender norms that had been set out for
women, I also resisted the sari: a symbol of everything that
I intended to challenge and stand firm against. But when
I first wore a sari, my mother helping me to choose one that
I liked and then draping it around me, it felt momentous
– as if she was sending me out into the big, wide world with
her love wrapped around me. I felt elegant and beautiful.
'You can't stomp around as you usually do – you are
a woman now', my mother had said with a laugh.

    In the north of India where I was born and grew up,
hijras wore saris too. *Hijras* are India's ancient transgender
community, the third gender, and even though their world
and mine were very separate, I would see them at weddings
and other auspicious occasions bringing music, dance and
joy. The sari for them is a badge of honour, a sign of their
womanhood, an armour against a world that tells them they
are not 'real women'. The sari marks their transition from
one gender to the other, a bold public proclamation of who
they truly are on the inside, the folds of the sari enfolding

Shepherd & Robertson, *Hijras*, 1862–4

them within this community where they feel their whole self for the first time.

Laxmi Narayan Tripathi, a well-known transgender activist from India, has spoken about how, when her mother bought her a sari, she knew for the first time that she had accepted Laxmi completely as a woman. In an article for the online platform Border&Fall, she also says, 'Sari is my culture, sari is my soul, sari is my religion. It enhances the femininity of the Indian body. It has always been the medium through which we express our femininity, our tradition, our culture ...'[1]

And even as the sari has become associated with womanhood, if we look back into history, we see that the practice of wearing unstitched clothing draped around the body was not limited to women. Statues from the Indus Valley Civilisation found in Harappa and Mohenjo-daro in northern India show men and women wearing long strips of fabric draped over one shoulder.[2] During the Mauryan period (around 300 BCE), we see sculptures of men and women wearing rectangular pieces of fabric on the lower parts of the body, a freeing and unconstrained garment irrespective of gender.

The modern drape of the sari (and accompanying blouse), known as the Nivi drape, was popularised during colonial times by the Victorians, who imposed repressive ideas of feminine modesty on women. Women in parts of India in the late 1800s still wore the sari without a blouse or a choli, going bare-breasted. But the British had their own ideas of modesty, refusing club entry to Indian women who didn't wear a shirt or a blouse under the sari. Colonial expansion relied on ideas of moral uprightness and superiority that shifted notions of 'propriety' in India, with gender norms becoming more rigid and hierarchical. Even as Indians overthrew colonial rule, this legacy has persisted – now deeply embedded in society. Men still wear a similar unstitched garment in many parts of the Indian subcontinent, calling it a lungi, dhoti or *veshti*. Both the sari and the dhoti consist of long strips of unstitched cloth, but they take on completely different meanings depending on the wearer and the drape: the sari becomes feminine, while the dhoti embodies masculinity. The way the sari was interpreted and worn has changed over time and gradually, as the gendered rules and expectations became more entrenched in society, the sari has become a symbol of these codes.

When we assign a value of womanhood or femininity to an inanimate object such as the sari, we automatically ascribe to it the cultural and social expectations associated with these labels. Recently, however, efforts have been made to untie the sari from the bonds of societal preconceptions around what a sari wearer should look like and represent, taking it forward into a modern world where

Priest-King, Indus Valley Civilisation, c.2000–1900 BCE

gender binaries are less polarised. The implicit associations of the sari with 'feminine' values are now being challenged, and social media in particular has democratised attempts to free the sari from gendered tropes. Wearers are taking back power by adapting the sari to their lifestyle and embodying their whole, expansive identities.

Oorbee Roy, known as @auntyskates on Instagram, pairs the sari with trainers and T-shirts. She is seen exploding on to our grids on a skateboard, creating an apparent dissonance between the role that a traditional housewife – a mother in a sari – has been expected to play and a pursuit that is still considered mostly masculine.[3] She is also breaking ageist stereotypes since skating is typically seen as a youthful pursuit, not something a middle-aged woman is expected to enjoy – or be good at. Elsewhere, Pushpak Sen regularly posts pictures of himself wearing a sari on Instagram (@thebongmunda), having gained a considerable following with his hashtag #SariNotSorry. In his many posts, Pushpak insists that the sari doesn't have anything to do with gender or sexuality. Instead, it is its aesthetics and heritage that make it so special, and everyone should have access to saris. This more expansive mode of relating to the sari is visible too in the work of Alok Vaid-Menon, a gender non-conforming artist and creator of #DeGenderFashion, who is often seen in saris on their Instagram (@alokvmenon). There are more than a hundred ways to drape a sari and, in this sense, the sari becomes the person wearing it. It can be versatile, adaptable, fluid. Although women of all shapes and sizes have been wearing the sari for centuries, recently it has been adopted as a symbol of body positivity. Influencer and digital creator Sobia Ameen (@sobia93), for instance, fuses her urban identity with tradition, using the sari to rediscover her identity as a Bangladeshi woman and break taboos around body shapes and sizes in the fashion industry.

Chantal Garcia, Oorbee Roy (aka Aunty Skates), 2021

Elsewhere, designers are bringing traditional weaves into their designs, celebrating the rich legacy of Indian crafts-manship while also reconfiguring the sari into innovative silhouettes that represent a more liberated, independent woman. Shilpa Chavan, the acclaimed designer behind the label Little Shilpa, showcased her collection Grey Matters in 2013 at London Fashion Week – where she envisioned the sari at the intersection of the modern and the traditional, using conventional masculine forms in her designs. Here, saris were coupled with shirts and bow ties, worn decon-structed as a kilt with military headwear, fluidly moving between Eastern and Western shapes, shattering the divide between feminine and masculine. The sari is empowered and bold, strutting and taking control, challenging its association with passivity and subservience. Mavuri, a hand-loom sari brand from Andhra Pradesh in southeast India, recently launched a campaign called 'Beyond Binaries' to showcase the sari's fluidity. Men – and women – no longer have to reconfigure their bodies to wear the sari, and people of all identities are establishing the idea that it can be a practical garment, detaching it from restrictive labels such as 'pretty', 'graceful' or 'elegant'.

A sari, in its unstitched form, adapts to the size we are, whether small, big, tall, short. We are not reduced to our measurements as is the case with other clothing. I do not have to think of whether a sari will fit me or not when I am buying one, and I can happily pass it on to my children just as I can wear saris that have been passed on to me through preceding generations – the weave of the sari carrying the memories and experiences, the wisdom of those who wore it before me. I do not have to think of dieting or squeezing myself into the measurements that a designer has deemed acceptable, those strictures of darns and tacks that force me to think about how big my waist is or how wide my hips are. The sari flows around me, enveloping me in its voluptuousness and sensuality, and I make it my own just the way I am: ambivalent, mutable, unfixed.

Contemporary designers continue to play with the pre-draped sari form. Designer Tarun Tahiliani has created a lehenga–sari hybrid that can be worn pre-stitched and fastened with a zip. This pre-pleated form has made the sari more accessible and attractive to younger women, who saw the traditional sari as time-consuming, not fitting into their busy lifestyles. And this type of sari can have pockets! The social enterprise AseemShakti from Mumbai has designed a pre-draped 'instant' sari with invisible pockets that is striving to establish the sari as workwear for women of all ages. This instant sari can be worn within thirty seconds and does not even require an underskirt or petticoat, which can feel cumbersome during the hot, humid months of the year. The sari thus sheds its image of docility and compliance, symbolising a more galvanised woman forging an independent persona.

The rigid, binary constraints of femininity and masculinity box all of us into certain archetypal behaviours. If we are to move beyond this, it is important to challenge the way femininity is codified as performance in certain objects, such as the sari, when it is forcing the wearer to embody narrow notions of womanhood rather than allowing for an unrestrained existence. This requires us to examine our own internalised preconceptions of who a sari wearer ought to be, and what they represent, while questioning and challenging the externalised societal expectations imposed on all of us from a young age: those that tell us how to be a man or a woman, that we have to choose one

Little Shilpa, The Raj Kilt, 2014

or the other and how to fit into these identities that have been predetermined for us. We will then see that a woman does not have to be passive, subservient and demure; neither is a sari supposed to be old-fashioned, traditional, feminine and all the other labels we have subconsciously assigned to it.

The malleability of the sari makes it the perfect vehicle for asserting individuality. To drape the sari to complement your body is to express your identity and your emotions – and to fit it around what you want to be, what you want to do. It doesn't expect the wearer to be anything they don't want to be to fit into it, or force them to squeeze into any narrow confines. For some, it can be a way of articulating their whole identity and overcoming dysphoria, creating a sense of belonging within a femininity that aligns with their inner self, while for others it can mean dismantling binary constructs completely. And, for some others, it is a way of stepping boldly outside the passive and subservient notions of womanhood that they have felt forced into. The sari in its unstitched form – with no hems, buttons, or zips – is an opportunity to break free of the limiting gendered associations that women – and men – are often confined by, both emotionally and physically. In this way, the sari becomes a proclamation of freedom and self-expression, embracing ourselves and our bodies in all their capacious glory.

1   Aarti Betigeri, 'Dress & Identity', Border & Fall, www.borderandfall.com/journal/dress-identity/ [Accessed 8 January 2023]
2   A Bronze Age civilisation in northwest India between about 3300 and 1300 BCE. It was one of the earliest civilisations, along with ancient Egypt and Mesopotamia. The statue *Priest-King*, now in the National Museum in New Delhi, shows the trefoil drape over one shoulder seen during the Gandhara period (first millennium BCE to second millennium CE). This Graeco-Indian period is the first in which we start seeing more elaborate drapes that resemble the sari today.
3   While many more women are now skateboarding, they are still very much in the minority – with women being only about twenty-three per cent of the total skateboarding population in the USA.

Himanshu
Verma

Interviewed by Amardeep Singh Dhillon

As a curator, collector and wearer of saris, Himanshu Verma is interested
in the garment's fluidity and ambiguity. He first began draping the sari
in 2006 as a form of androgynous play with gender stereotypes. Since
then, Verma has witnessed a dramatic shift in the relationship of younger
generations across South Asia to the sari – particularly in the spheres of
street style and social media. From researching and writing about the sari
to being photographed wearing it, his critical re-evaluation of the garment
has played a pivotal role in this shift.

In 2012, Verma founded The Saree Festival, a series of exhibitions, film
screenings and talks that examine the continued cultural relevance of
the sari. Starting in New Delhi, the festival spread across India – travelling
to Mumbai, Chennai and Hyderabad – underlining Verma's dedication
to instigating conversations about the beauty of the draped, unstitched
cloth. Here, he is interviewed by writer and activist Amardeep Singh
Dhillon about masculinity, spirituality and the impact of colonial rule
on the way Indians dress.

RIGHT   Himanshu Verma at The Saree Festival, Alliance
          Française de Delhi, New Delhi, 2016
OVERLEAF Himanshu Verma, *Lad Holding Marigold-Ball*
          (*After The Coquette by Raja Ravi Varma*), 2013

AMARDEEP SINGH DHILLON
When did you first start wearing
the sari?

HIMANSHU VERMA   I started
wearing the sari mainly within the
art community, mostly to openings and then in collaboration
with photographers. I was reading
work by Emma Tarlo, a British
anthropologist who describes
how Indian men gave up their
traditional costumes in response
to the challenge of being a 'man',
in the modern sense of the word,
under the colonial project.[1] Those
thoughts were swimming in my
head as I was wondering what
to wear to the opening of an
exhibition, so I decided to reclaim
the sari as a masculine garment.
That's when I first draped the sari.

ASD   Has wearing the sari
changed how you express
your gender?

HV   Personally, I feel that the
sari goes beyond gender. In
some ways, the sari is also
beyond politics – at least for me.
It's a garment of self-expression
and aesthetic pleasure that
allows me to engage with India's
textile history. I wouldn't say
that my own gender identity has
particularly changed through
wearing the sari, although I do
consider it a very spiritual act.
Drapes themselves are pretty
gender neutral, though of course
they tend to signify a softness
that may be understood as
feminine. But the very fact that
we might conceive of 'softness'
as something feminine in the
first place emerges from a very
particular contemporary understanding of gender.

ASD   In terms of masculinity
having been constructed in
opposition to a certain kind of
softness, it's interesting that
these divisions between gender
traits calcified under British colonial rule. Would men have worn
the sari prior to colonisation?

HV   With the arrival of the
sultanates and the Islamic
dynasties, there was a departure
from drapes and an adoption of
stitched clothing. At that time,
even stitched clothing was pretty
amorphous. There weren't any

binary distinctions between what
men and women should wear, in
terms of structured lines – that
came in later with the British.
Before then, garments were very
fluid, very flowing. In some ways,
the British Empire enforced the
idea that Indian men were not
manly enough, and they respond-
ed to it by changing their mode of
dress and behaviour. It was part
of a larger project of overhauling
Indian society. Although the
contemporary drape of the sari,
which evolved in the nineteenth
century, is typically worn by

women, if you look at older
drapes – especially regional
drapes – there is a large crossover between the sari and the
dhoti (the sari being a one-piece
garment, and the dhoti a two-
piece garment for men).

ASD   The construction of masculinity is particularly important
in India currently, with the development of the Hindutva project.
This form of ethno-nationalism
relies on the consolidation of a
particular form of maleness. Con-
sidering that context, what are the
implications of men playing with
the kind of aesthetics of softness
that might be coded as feminine?

HV   When you talk about
softness, there's this sense
of how men 'used' to dress.
However, inside religious spaces,
for instance, there's a code for
priests, who are supposed to
wear unstitched clothing. This is
still observed in very traditional
temples. When a priest is serving
Krishna, he wears dhotis and
drapes, which are deliberately not
ironed as a marker of purity. He
also always goes veiled in these
spaces, which in another space
would be seen as very feminine.
I'm not sure if right-wing Hindutva
activists are in tune with that aesthetic of masculinity. Their kind
of masculinity is very aggressive,
and based on a binary division
of Hindus versus the other.

ASD   How have reactions to you
and other men experimenting
with the sari changed in the
past fifteen years, since you first
started wearing it?

HV   For me, how people react
has never been a concern, though

THE OFFBEAT SARI

I do try to observe it. In general, I've not really come across any malicious intent or rudeness as such, except for a few people now and then calling me names. And that really reflects their insecurity. Largely the reaction to me wearing a sari is one of curiosity, which is very endearing and charming. When I first started The Saree Festival, there weren't that many sari projects around, so it was pioneering in some respects. Now there's an overwhelming barrage of sari culture on social media, which I can't really identify with.

ASD   Where do you think this explosion in urban sari culture comes from? And why has it become something you don't identify with?

HV   It coincided with the rise of social media. Perhaps the sari's streetwear comeback reflects the sense of nostalgia and disconnect we feel from our traditions ... ? The numbers of sari wearers are constantly falling, as more and more people give it up for other sartorial options. It's being phased out of women's everyday wardrobes but its visibility is constantly increasing in urban contexts – often among a very limited elitist, social-media-savvy demographic that is still a minority. There's this whole 'sari influencer' trend, which is completely unbearable sometimes! I've always been wary of flaunting the sari online. I'm not interested in posting pictures of me wearing it, and I don't feel any pressure to be 'on top' of this whole game, because there are so many men wearing saris right now.

ASD   How would you describe your style?

HV   I'm largely drawn to everyday saris: cotton drapes with a minimal pattern, which are in some ways more conventionally masculine although women often wear them as a standard. A simple sari with a plain body and border, akin to a dhoti, is also very versatile. I feel a certain comfort with the regular Nivi drape, which is very urbane and sophisticated. Personally, I love inventing new drapes as I wear the sari. One of my favourites is a cross between the Nauvari and the Nivi drape, which provides more room to negotiate the spaces between masculine and feminine.

ASD   You use the term 'spiritual' to describe your relationship with the sari. What do you mean by that?

HV   Well, especially if you look at the religious aspect of the drapes, there's that whole aesthetic of purity, which the sari is a marker of. But it also has to do with what you feel like when you wear it. The sari is literally an all-covering drape – it envelops you in its embrace. There are so many ways to play with the drape, and that reflects what you're feeling on a particular day – whether you're sad, happy, excited ... if you're going crazy, you tend to hold your sari in a different way. In that sense, it's a garment that perhaps allows you to be more aware of yourself, because the way you drape a sari helps to centre your energy. The way it covers you from head to toe, and touches the ground,

roots you to the Earth in some metaphorical way. However, the sari is a garment that also has immense élan – it allows you to fly!

1   See Emma Tarlo, *Clothing Matters: Dress and Identity in India* (Chicago, IL: Chicago University Press, 1996).

Sara Hylton, *The Demigods of Mumbai* series, 2017–ongoing. Rajni and Puja wait for the train at the Bandra station in Mumbai

Sunil Gupta and Charan Singh, *Rizwan #2, Delhi: Communities of Belonging* series, 2017

Sara Hylton, *The Demigods of Mumbai* series, 2017–ongoing. *Hijras* near their shared settlement outside of the Mahim train station

ABOVE   Sara Hylton, *The Demigods of Mumbai* series, 2017–ongoing. Radhika, originally from Andhra Pradesh, performs a blessing on public transport

OVERLEAF   Sunil Gupta, *Untitled #13*, *The New Pre-Raphaelites* series, 2008

THE OFFBEAT SARI

Manou, 2020. Portrait of Caroline Zeliang

Saurabh Dasgupta, 2019. Portrait of Mamta Sharma Das

ABOVE   Abdullah Usman Khan, 2014. Portrait of Mithu Sen
OVERLEAF   India Hobson, 2019. Portrait of Meara Sharma for *Vogue India*

THE OFFBEAT SARI

ABOVE   Rema Chaudary, 2021. Portrait of Ṛta Kapur Chishti for *Architectural Digest*
RIGHT   Pulkit Mishra, 2020. Portrait of Beenu Mishra

WEARERS

Endless creativity in styling saris – from everyday wearers through to
fashion bloggers and influential public figures – is revealed through a
range of platforms, including art photography and print media, showing
that the future of the sari is bold, undaunted and defined by individual
flair. The imagination of these wearers is fuelled and documented by
social media, where people of all ages across South Asia and beyond
share their mix-and-match outfits.

ABOVE Randhir Singh, 2022. Portrait of Monika Correa
LEFT   Rishabh, 2020. Portrait of Anima Raani Das

RESISTANCE

IV

Radical Disobedience

Sonia Faleiro

One afternoon in August 1976, a group of women in saris walked out of the Grunwick photo-processing factory in Willesden, north London. At the head of the group was Jayaben Desai, a fiery Gujarati who had arrived in the country eight years earlier. That afternoon, Desai's line manager had compared the predominantly South Asian female workforce to monkeys. An outraged Desai shot back: 'What you're running here is not a factory, it is a zoo. There are many types of animals in a zoo. Some are monkeys who dance to your tune, others are lions who can bite your head off. We are those lions, Mr Manager. I have had enough – I want my freedom!'[1]

Desai's demand that the women of Grunwick be allowed to join a workers' union to receive the same workplace guarantees as their white male counterparts captured the national imagination. The media referred to her group as the 'Strikers in Saris'. Thousands of people showed their support by participating in mass pickets. It would be two years until the women's demand was met, but the Grunwick protest is now celebrated as a turning point in Britain's trade-union history. And the sari was viewed as a symbol of resistance, not unlike the white garments of the suffragettes and the berets of the Black Panther Party.

One particularly striking image of Desai hangs in the National Portrait Gallery in London. Taken by David Mansell two months after the strike began, it depicts her gazing up at a wall of stern-faced police officers. She appears tiny. She wears stud earrings, a knitted cardigan covered with protest badges and slim bangles, and we see a glimpse of her printed sari. A black leather handbag dangles from her narrow wrist. She should be concerned, but her expression is merely curious, as though wondering why these police officers – or really anyone at all – would take her on. 'They wanted to break us down', she reflected shortly before her death in 2010. 'But we did not break'.[2]

It was hardly a surprise to learn that Desai had participated in India's freedom struggle as a teenager.[3] Mahatma

David Mansell, 1977. Jayaben Desai at the Grunwick film-processing plant in Willesden, Brent

Gandhi with Sarojini Naidu before departure for England, 1931

Gandhi's decision to wear the simplest of homespun khadi was as much an attempt to boycott English-made goods as it was a means of visual resistance. Many of the leading female figures of the movement, such as the poet Sarojini Naidu, had studied abroad – Naidu attended King's College London and Cambridge University – and were comfortable in Western wear but, having decided to devote themselves to the civil-resistance movement, they followed in Gandhi's footsteps, wearing homespun cotton saris.

The newly independent nation founded in 1947 now had its own culture and history of protest. Gandhian values of inclusivity and non-violence inspired many women, not all of whom came from means, to stand up publicly for what they believed. By wearing the sari, these women asserted their identity and demanded respect for their values and culture. Saris were functional, adaptable and cheap, making them the most effective form of wearable protest in a country like India.

In the early 1970s, a group of villagers in the Himalayas banded together to protest against the commercial forestry that was depriving them of their forest-based livelihoods. Women played a vital role in the movement. The protest became widely known after several of them were captured in a now iconic image of them hugging a tree, with saris wrapped around their waists, to protect it from loggers. It came to be referred to as the Chipko ('Embrace') Movement and is now regarded as the country's first large-scale ecological protest.

Two decades later, the social worker Medha Patkar started the Narmada Bachao Andolan (Save the Narmada Movement) to stop a dam being built on the Narmada River that would render about 20,000 people, mostly of indigenous origin, utterly homeless. Patkar mobilised peaceful protests for which she was repeatedly beaten by the police and thrown into jail. Like the women of Chipko, Patkar's clothes came to symbolise the integrity of her intentions. She was viewed as trustworthy because of the simplicity of what she wore. Although Patkar did not belong to the communities she was fighting for, by living with them, working alongside them and dressing like them, she was viewed as one of them. The role of saris in this show of solidarity cannot be underestimated. 'Her threadbare khadi sari only emphasises her frailness', reported *India Today* in 1991, after Patkar was awarded Sweden's prestigious Right Livelihood Award. 'Yet beneath the fragile exterior lies a woman of steel'. [4]

By the 2000s, women in saris had played a role in the most prominent protests in India. As India modernised and liberalised, as the economy boomed and the country changed, seemingly for the better, one of the things that

Joerg Boethling, 2002. Medha Patkar, Arundhati Roy and Domkhedi villagers protesting against the construction of a dam on the Narmada River

unfortunately remained much the same was the position of women. The country was still deeply patriarchal. Women had far fewer educational and career opportunities than men, and they were also subject to high levels of violence. It was clear that the struggle for women's rights would be prolonged and fierce, and that it would be led by women – men simply had too much to lose. Non-violence was no longer seen as productive, and the presence of women added an edge to the protests. A spirit of vigilantism bubbled to the fore.

Perhaps no one epitomises this new wave of protests better than the Gulabi Gang, a group of women who first came together in 2006 in the northern Indian state of Uttar Pradesh. They became famous for strutting around and thrashing misbehaving men with long bamboo poles.

The women are led by Sampat Pal Devi, the daughter of a shepherd who was married off when she was a child of twelve to a twenty-year-old ice-cream vendor with whom she went on to have five children. In her telling, she was prompted to stand up for women's rights after observing a man beating his wife. An outraged Pal mustered a gang of women to give the man a taste of his own medicine.

We know the beating achieved the desired outcome because Pal then decided to make the group official. In a society where men thought they owned women and the police couldn't be bothered to provide relief, only women – and vigilantes, at that – could protect themselves and others. 'Mind you,' Pal told the BBC's Soutik Biswas in 2007, 'we are not a gang in the usual sense of the term. We are a gang for justice.'[5]

The Gulabi Gang derived its name from the fluorescent pink saris worn by its members. In her biography of the group, the journalist Amana Fontanella-Khan writes that Pal had briefly considered asking the women to wear badges so that they were easily identifiable in public, but that idea was rejected in favour of saris. Pal decided on pink because it was free of caste or religious associations.[6] '"When we go anywhere people will be curious," Sampat said, clapping her hands in delight. "They'll be even more afraid of us in uniforms!"'[7]

Pal's decision to dress herself and her fellow gang members in saris made a difference to how they were perceived. In those who had reason to be afraid, the Gulabi Gang inspired fear – but as news of the gang spread across India, the image of the women in their saris, with bamboo sticks in hand and ferocious expressions stamped on their faces, inspired sympathy and admiration.

Six years later, on a cold December night in 2012, a twenty-three-year-old medical student named Jyoti Singh was returning home from the cinema in Delhi when she

Joerg Boethling, 2019. The Gulabi Gang

was raped and tortured by six men in a moving bus. Singh's death a few days later triggered the largest protest against sexual violence that India had ever seen. In Delhi, where the protestors gathered before the Presidential Palace, they were met by riot police who attempted to disperse them with batons, water cannons and tear gas. Although this protest was notable for the participation of men, it played a vital role in reiterating that women could and must stand up for their rights.

About two years later, I had the opportunity to see the impact that the Delhi protest had had on ordinary people. In the summer of 2014, two teenage girls were found hanging from a mango tree in the orchard of their village of Katra Sadatganj in Uttar Pradesh. Someone in the village had taken a picture of the hanging girls and, after it found its way to Twitter, there was an uproar. A rumour circulated that they had been raped and killed by dominant-caste men who were said to have hanged the bodies on public property as a boast that they had nothing to fear – either from the villagers, who were lower caste, or from the police, who tended to side with dominant and upper-caste groups.

In ordinary circumstances, in a state like Uttar Pradesh, the police would have taken down the bodies and had them cremated, forgoing an investigation on the excuse that there was no need. On this occasion, however, they were prevented from a potential cover-up by the mothers of the two girls. Joined by their mother-in-law, the women in saris sat at the foot of the tree and refused to let the police come close.

News of the women's radical disobedience attracted journalists, who rushed to the village to capture this moment of unheard-of subversion. These were women who didn't speak in the presence of men, who didn't eat until all the men and boys in the family had eaten, and yet here they were staring down dozens of police officers.

When I met the mothers for the first time in 2015, I was struck by their determination. They had wanted justice, but didn't have the money or clout to make it happen. What they did have was the power to protest – and so, silently and non-violently, the women had settled down to ask for what they deserved, which was a thorough investigation into the deaths of their children.

The impact of their protest has continued to be felt in the decade that followed. Five years later, in September 2020, another group of women gathered in response to the government's decision to privatise the agricultural market. Hundreds of thousands of farmers drove their tractors and trucks to the national capital in a declaration of protest.

Critics argued that the decision to involve women was designed to protect the men from police action. But this statement ignores the fact that women play a vital role in agriculture, comprising seventy-five per cent of the rural workforce according to Oxfam.[8] With their saris pulled up and their dupattas secured firmly around their waists, women are as much a part of the Indian farmstead as any man. Despite this, only thirteen per cent of them own any land, according to a study by the Center for Land Governance.[9]

The women who joined the protest had another agenda besides the stated one. 'I joined [this protest] so people know that we are also farmers', said Sunita Rani, a farmer from Haryana state, in an interview with *Reuters*.[10] Kavita Kumari echoed the sentiment: 'I have been a farmer since I was a child … I can ride a bike, and a tractor. People will see if we can come forward for protests, we can also do farming'.[11]

This time, the protestors were able to claim victory. Two months after they rolled into Delhi, the government agreed to scrap the proposed legislation.[12] Images of the farmers celebrating were broadcast across India. They distributed sweetmeats, played music, danced and waved flags. But the sweetest victory of all may have belonged to the women in saris – recognised finally for the role they played not just in feeding the country but also transforming it.

1   David Mansell, 'Jayaben Desai', *National Portrait Gallery*, 23 October 1977, www.npg.org.uk/collections/search/person/mp160854/jayaben-desai [Accessed 15 November 2022]

2   'Strikers in saris', *Guardian* (20 January 2010), www.theguardian.com/society/gallery/2010/jan/20/grunwick-strike-women [Accessed 18 November 2022]

3   Jayaben Desai, Working Class Movement Library, www.wcml.org.uk/our-collections/activists/jayaben-desai/ [Accessed 18 November 2022]

4   Uday Mahurkar, 'Narmada Bachao Andolan crusader Medha Patkar gains recognition at last', *India Today* (15 December 1991), www.indiatoday.in/magazine/states/story/19911215-narmada-bachao-andolan-crusader-medha-patkar-gains-recognition-at-last-815239-1991-12-14 [Accessed 9 January 2023]

5   Soutik Biswas, 'India's "pink" vigilante women', BBC News (26 November 2007), http://news.bbc.co.uk/2/hi/7068875.stm [Accessed 15 November 2022]

6   The colour saffron, for example, is associated with Hinduism, whereas green is supposed to have been the Prophet Muhammad's favourite colour. Blue is associated with the Hindu deity Lord Krishna.

7   Amana Fontanella-Khan, *Pink Sari Revolution: a tale of women and power in India* (New York, NY: W. W. Norton, 2013), 22.

8   Urvi Shrivastav, 'Women in Agriculture: the potential and gaps', *Business World* (5 January 2021), www.businessworld.in/article/Women-In-Agriculture-The-Potential-And-Gaps/05-01-2021-361877 [Accessed 15 November 2022]

9   Bhasker Tripathi, 'Lakshadweep, Meghalaya Have Most Women Land Holders; Punjab, West Bengal Fewest', *IndiaSpend* (19 February 2018), www.indiaspend.com/lakshadweep-meghalaya-have-most-women-land-holders-punjab-west-bengal-fewest-54024/ [Accessed 10 January 2023]

10   Roli Srivastava, 'India's "invisible" women hope for recognition at farmers protests', *Reuters* (16 December 2020), www.reuters.com/article/india-women-farmers-idAFL8N2IV4M5 [Accessed 15 November 2022]

11   Ibid.

12   Esha Mitra and Rhea Mogul, 'Indian farmers forced Modi to back down on new laws. So why aren't they going home?', *CNN* (26 November 2021), www.edition.cnn.com/2021/11/26/india/india-farmers-protest-one-year-intl-hnk-dst [Accessed 15 November 2022]

NORBLACK
NORWHITE

Mriga Kapadiya and Amrit Kumar interviewed by Dal Chodha

Blazing a trail through the scene since 2010, fashion brand NORBLACK NORWHITE (NBNW) combine a desire to preserve regional Indian textiles, and nostalgia for 1990s hip-hop, with contemporary silhouettes that resist stereotypes of Indian identity and dress. At the helm are Mriga Kapadiya and Amrit Kumar, both of whom were raised in Toronto and moved to Mumbai in 2010, before later settling in New Delhi.

NBNW operates across fashion and art, instigating narrative-led design collaborations with brands such as adidas, Fila and Air Canada. The studio aims to forge links with subcultures and build communities by 'sharing indigenous skills and stories' and connecting to their roots, drawing on an eclectic design language built from streetwear, film and childhood memories. Recognised across the global diaspora as disruptors, NBNW's work has been featured in *Wallpaper** and *i-D* magazines, and showcased at the V&A and the Textile Museum of Canada. Here, they are in conversation about their practice with fashion writer Dal Chodha, editor-in-chief of *Archivist Addendum*.

RIGHT   Bikramjit Bose, 2020. NORBLACK NORWHITE, hand-painted chiffon saris, Holidaze collection
OVERLEAF   Bharat Sikka, 2020. Portrait of NORBLACK NORWHITE

DAL CHODHA   This is the third time that your work has been presented within a museum context – how do you feel about that?

MRIGA KAPADIYA   It's exciting! Early on, we were invited to be part of a show at the V&A and, to be honest, we didn't really understand how prestigious that was. Prior to that, we'd shown at the Textile Museum of Canada too, and so slowly we have come to realise that museums understand what we are doing. Museums put things into perspective, and it's meant that our work is reaching an audience outside of India, which in turn means we are always asking ourselves questions about how we present – and represent – what we do.

DC   When you first moved to Mumbai from Toronto in 2010, you both talked about wanting to explore your own roots and look less through a diasporic lens. What lessons do you think you've learned?

AMRIT KUMAR   I've been living in India full-time for the last thirteen years now, but what I expected before moving here was different to the reality. Growing up, I never visited India, so whatever I saw in films – or the saris my mum kept packed in suitcases for special occasions – was really all I knew. Coming here, I learned about the culture of the sari – all the different ways it is worn, interpreted, understood. I'm Sikh, so my mum wore a lot of salwar kameezes, and so my relationship with the sari is different to Mriga's.

MK   My mum is south Indian, and my dad is Gujarati. Growing up, I have a very clear image in my head of my mum wearing simple cotton saris when we would visit Hyderabad every summer. I loved watching her move in them with such ease. Outside of India, her saris were in a heavier silk and only really worn to shows, concerts, parties and dinners – it wasn't everyday wear. I grew up surrounded by a range of saris, but the way they were worn was very specific: classic over the one shoulder with the pleats done

a certain way. When we moved to India, we spent time observing the million different ways it is worn and how it is a political thing. We learned about those nuances from being in India.

DC   What kind of politics did you unpack?

MK   Like all clothing, it is intrinsically linked to class and social status – and culture. Amrit and I would gravitate towards certain styles and people would say, 'Oh you cannot wear that ... that is for

this type of person.' So we were able to observe the class politics at play, while also learning how the sari changes across the country. All saris are not equal.

DC   Before you decided to move to India, what were your earliest memories of the sari?

AK   I was four years old when I saw my mum in a sari for the first time. I vividly remember the exact sari and the process of her turning the pleats. Another memory I have is when I got to wear one for the first time, when I was around sixteen. I was probably going to a party with a friend, but I remember feeling like I was entering womanhood because of this confidence that a sari gives you. You walk differently; you feel different.

DC   Is the sari a kind of coming-of-age garment?

MK   Absolutely, I think so. I don't have a clear vision of when I first saw the sari, because it was always around. I did think of it like a rite of passage, however, because it just felt so feminine. As a kid, I was not sure I could pull that off – it was a very elegant and proper thing that I always felt intimidated by. Now, through our friends and the NBNW community, that's changed. There are so many new expressions of it.

DC   Was that your motivation for designing the hand-dyed cotton lurex Shimma Sari that you released in 2017? It was paired with a mesh blouse and made quite an impact when it was worn by actor Sonam Kapoor at Cannes.

THE OFFBEAT SARI

MK   We didn't do it that way intentionally to dismantle any of those social codes ... it just came very naturally. We wanted to make something fresh, comfortable and fun, which is our approach at NBNW. The blouse is essential – it puts the whole look together – and so the mesh was a no-brainer, because it makes you feel comfortable and confident. I feel like in Toronto – or maybe even outside of India – the sari is more sexualised and exoticised ... it becomes more complicated. We were interested in something more akin to streetwear.

AK   For a lot of diasporic people, our access to India was largely filtered through Bollywood. When we started NBNW, our research focused a lot on iconic actors and scenes from films, but we've moved away from that now.

DC   NBNW has naturally evolved into a cultural platform, and a lot of what you're working on now is about preserving and promoting indigenous skills and stories. The hand-painted Tulip Sari (2020) feels like a true expression of what you are trying to do.

MK   With that piece we wanted to riff off the iconic image of a white chiffon sari worn in the rain, which is such a classic Bollywood film scene. We wanted to use the chiffon in a much more colourful and playful way. The Tulip Sari is a very easy piece to wear – different to the Shimma, but they are both comfortable. We shot a group of our girlfriends in them just before the pandemic hit, and they each wore a different blouse and had their own style.

AK   Despite how comfortable and easy the Tulip Sari feels, each one is totally unique. Conceptually, it began as a scarf, and we spent one year developing the lengths of fabric with artisans in Delhi – partly in homage to Jaipur, which is known for its printed chiffon. But it is also as an expression of what NBNW is. One of our missions is to hold space to appreciate the complexities of what it means to make and work out of India, and this continues to grow. We haven't made another sari since.

Indian suffragettes during the Women's Coronation Procession, London, 1911

Pamela Singh, *Chipko Tree Huggers of the Himalayas #78*, 1994

Kasturba Gandhi, 1940s

ABOVE Women and children during the Salt March protests, 1930
RIGHT Margaret Bourke-White, photograph of Mahatma Gandhi with
       charkha spinning wheel, 1946

ABOVE   Mahatma Gandhi's charkha, 1948
OVERLEAF   Raghu Rai, Indira Gandhi at a Congress session, 1966

THE OFFBEAT SARI

Ekaya × Masaba, hand-woven Mustard Silk Sari with cherry-blossom motifs, 2019

THE OFFBEAT SARI

Ekaya × Masaba, hand-woven Pink Silk Sari
with cherry-blossom motifs, 2019

ABOVE   Ekaya × Masaba, hand-woven Green Silk Sari, 2019
OVERLEAF NORBLACK NORWHITE, hand-painted chiffon saris,
          Holidaze collection, 2020

EKAYA
     × MASABA

Designer Masaba Gupta and fashion brand Ekaya defied sari stereotypes when they launched their Banarasi collection with photographs
of women playing cricket. Threaded with gold and silver, the Banarasi
style is often associated with formality; the designers deliberately
overturned this by showing the sari in full movement. Across India,
saris are worn while performing activities such as farming or complex
dance moves, and even riding a bicycle. Drawing on these realities
and the inherent strength of the sari textile, designers are repositioning
the sari for athleticism.

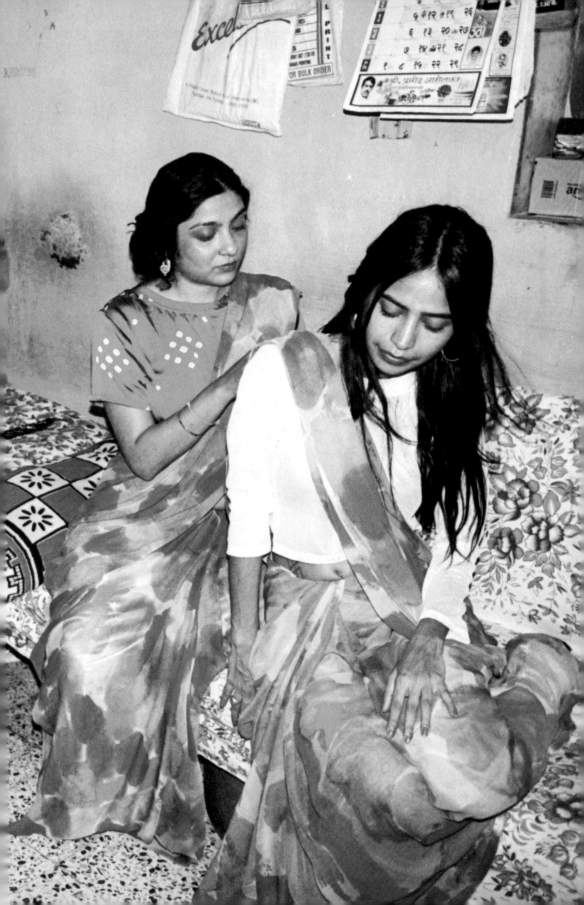

Anupam Nath, 2019. The Hargila Army

THE
      HARGILA ARMY
Can clothing help to save a bird from the brink of extinction? This
striking sari is part of the remarkable conservation success story of
the greater adjutant stork. By weaving stork motifs into saris, biologist
Purnima Devi Barman and the Hargila Army activist group in Assam
have transformed this threatened bird into a treasured local emblem.

A member of the Hargila Army displays a weave with motifs of the greater adjutant stork, 2017

ABOVE + TOP   Ravi Choudhary, 2017. Tamil Nadu farmers wearing saris during protests in Jantar Mantar

Joerg Boethling, 2009. The Gulabi Gang

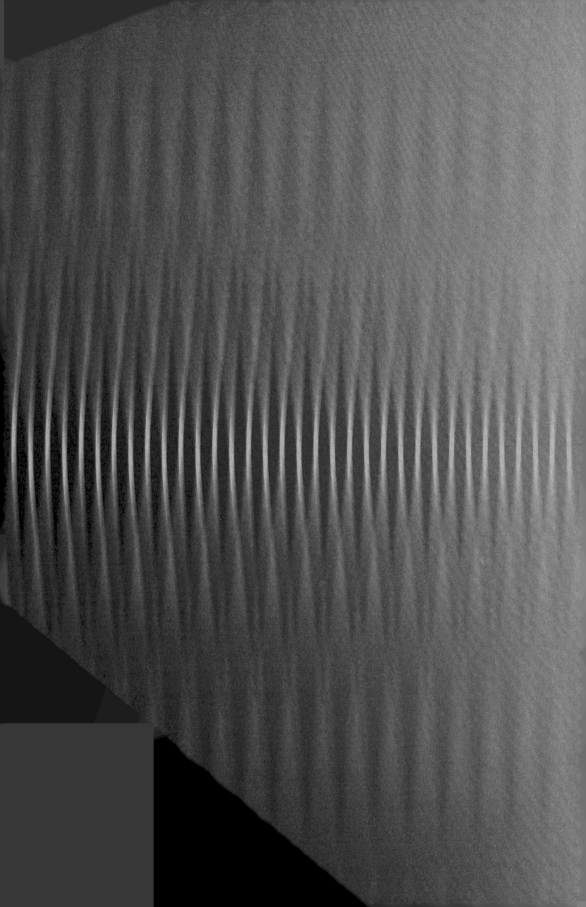

MATERIALITY

V

Crafting the Future

Tara Mayer

Like many women of her generation, my mother left rural Kerala to attend nursing school in north India, first in Patna and later in Delhi. It was the 1960s and India was changing rapidly. The country was industrialising and modernising, evolving in directions that were at once foreign and unmistakably her own. Yet, for those living within her shifting borders, India has always been changing, a land poised at the threshold of her own becoming. At seventeen years old, my mother was greeted by innumerable surprises and had to make innumerable adjustments. She applied the hesitant Hindi she had learned at school, purchased her first sweater to combat chilly north Indian winters, tore at chapatis in the college canteen while longing for rice. On a hard, general-class seat on Indian rail, she traversed nearly the full breadth of the subcontinent. She squinted and slept through lush hills and arid lowlands, places remade by recent history and yet obstinately unchanged.

In the North, she was overwhelmed by novelty. She adjusted and assimilated, laboured to fit in. To her relief, this was helped by her only clothing: two saris, in a modest and unassuming cotton hand-loom, which did nothing to betray her terrifying distance from home. To her surprise, fellow students occasionally mistook her for the advantaged daughter of an educated urban family, for whom khadi had become a fashionable emblem during these fresh decades of Indian independence: a sartorial selection steeped in political meaning.

Those of us outside India seeking better to understand the nuance and defiant hybridity of contemporary Indian fashion are often relegated to peering over a wall. First, we must contend with the maddening tenacity of colonial-era categories and assumptions, casting off a haunting anthropological gaze that obstructs, shrinks, reduces, snips, distorts and misaligns. In the late eighteenth and nineteenth century, European efforts to catalogue and record India's sartorial norms and practices formed part of a confluence

Frans Balthazar Solvyns, illustration from *The Costume of Indostan*, 1807

of knowledge-gathering projects.[1] Spanning disciplines as disparate as ethnography and physical geography, Europeans variously constructed notions of India's timelessness – of an eternal, unbroken and deeply Orientalised continuity. Such representations attest to the propensity for intellectual and aesthetic endeavours to intersect during the colonial period. An example is found in the work of Frans Balthazar Solvyns, the Flemish painter, printmaker and ethnographer. While living and working in India from 1791 to 1803, he drew an encyclopaedic body of portraits, which were subsequently etched and published in an influential collection called *The Costume of Indostan* (1807). Here, the everyday dress of Indians – a sphere that is gloriously contradictory, chaotic, subversive, porous and contingent – was rendered folkloric, almost static. Indian clothing became costume, neatly distilled and reduced, codified within the European imaginary.

There exists perhaps no better lens than cloth through which Indian self-conceptions of gender, class, modernity, history and place can be observed and experienced on their own terms. Enmeshed in the warp and weft of textile traditions that have emerged from antiquity lie many of the most tangible aspects of India's cultural innovation, creativity, technical skill and defiance. Nowhere is this more apparent than in the sari, the traditionally uncut cloth that is India's ubiquitous and iconic garment. If the sari's legacy dates back to the Indus Valley Civilisation some 5,000 years ago, then Indian weaving traditions boast an even more ancient history, having undergone incalculable evolutions and interpretations. Indian weavers have expertly clothed the bodies of multitudes, spanning millennia, from anonymous labourers to Mughal and European royalty. It is specifically through regional weaving techniques that the very finest Indian cloth is identified and for these techniques that it is prized. Silk saris from Benares (Banarasi) or Kanchipuram (Kanjeevaram) have been the most sought-after components of Indian wedding trousseaus for generations, along with diaphanous cottons from Dhaka (Dhakai or Jamdani), subtle cottons and silks from Kota in Rajasthan (Kota Doria), silk and cotton blends in the Chanderi weaves of Madhya Pradesh and countless others. Many weaving techniques – such as zari work, the addition of metallic threads to create intricate patterns usually on the borders and pallu of a sari – or ikat – a labour-intensive weaving and resist-dyeing technique – span regions, in riffs and variations too numerous to catalogue.

Through the depth and diversity of Indian weaving techniques, and the enduring expertise of Indian craft communities, contemporary designers are able to have even the most far-flung visions realised with absolute fidelity. Only in

India can textile innovations be hand-loomed efficiently on a one-off or minuscule scale, offering emerging designers the possibility of holding and touching their samples rather than relying on digital modelling – a privilege accessible to few outside the rarefied circles of French haute couture. David Abraham, Kevin Nigli and Rakesh Thakore, of contemporary Indian label Abraham & Thakore, have been pioneering this new chapter in Indian high fashion over recent decades, designing textiles and developing collections from an atelier in Noida in northern India. Theirs is a body of work that chronicles the emergence of the Indian fashion industry and, at the same time, illustrates the challenges, risks and reimaginings that arise when Indian designers draw both from international experiences and from perspectives that are deeply personal and idiosyncratic. Responding to a question about the archetypical 'A&T woman', the designers said:

> Fashion is a manifestation of identity, and for many of us in India today we constantly negotiate a path that balances several identities, traditional and modern. We believe that they are simply two aspects of the same persona. Having said that, our customers for the same leopard skin sari have ranged from one of the coolest young fashion models to an older professional, a mother of high school children.[2]

The leopard-motif sari was woven, not printed, from a wild and uncultivated tussore silk. Balancing tradition and modernity, and often blurring the distinctions between them, A&T likewise disrupt historical and conventional associations of khadi with austere and muted cotton through their hand-loomed saris, which are woven using a glistening metallic foil.

Modernity versus tradition is not the only dichotomy that is routinely overturned in the context of Indian fashion. Most Indian designers do not adhere to the global, mass-production models of fast fashion advanced by Europe-based Zara, H&M and Topshop; Japan-based UNIQLO; and China-based SHEIN, among others. The UN Alliance for Sustainable Fashion estimates that 'the fashion industry is a $2.4 trillion global industry that employs approximately 300 million people across the value chain – many of whom are women – and the scale of the industry is only expected to grow over the coming years'.[3] In its current form, the global fashion industry is environmentally extractive, socially exploitative and ecologically catastrophic.

While in recent decades South Asia has become a hub for global fast-fashion factories whose hiring and labour practices exploit a tangible economic need, a range of

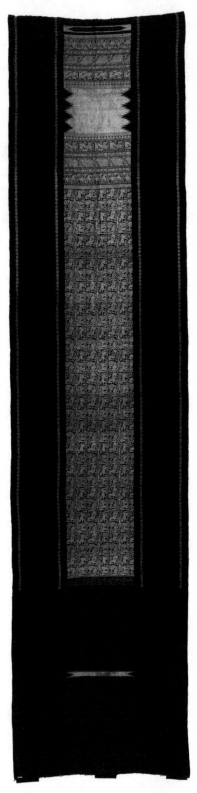

Silk sari from Benares, c. 19th century

Indian designers has emerged concurrently whose focus is on sustainability and craft stewardship. Bengali designer Sabyasachi Mukherjee, for example, has built a booming business based on traditional craft techniques that meaningfully support the livelihoods of the weavers he employs. As an extension of this, his 'Save the Sari' project is a non-profit endeavour started in 2013 to popularise regional weaves and offer a reliable point of sale in his stores without any additional markup. Sabyasachi Mukherjee, Abraham & Thakore and many other Indian designers work intimately with their own in-house systems of weavers and *kaarigars* (artisans) as well as suppliers.

In India, the historical anonymity of individual weavers and craftspeople is embedded within a tradition more inclined to recognise the artistic and creative achievements of whole communities or guilds. While individual craftspeople seldom attain the high profile or name-recognition status of certain Indian designers, there often exists a level of interdependency, symbiosis and lateral collaboration within these systems that differs fundamentally from models of fast fashion. Added to this is an endemic tradition of upcycling and repurposing. Saris are not thrown away, but mended, cut and reworked, reimagined and reincarnated. An ethos of sustainability is likewise present in the philosophical and spiritual tenets of *ahimsa*, of doing no harm, that goes beyond the environmental lip service, or greenwashing, prevalent within the global fashion industry.

Colour is the most widely acknowledged yet least understood facet of the sari's special character and of the evolution of Indian textiles more generally. Dye was produced and mastered in the subcontinent earlier and on a wider scale than almost anywhere else. For thousands of years, natural pigments were made by crushing soil, clay and rock to produce vibrant hues; insects were gathered for their colour-staining properties; and a vast array of plants were harvested and cultivated expressly for their depth and richness of colour. In addition to being environmentally safe, natural dyes proffer a profound and poetic rebuttal to the indistinguishable mimicry and fungibility of fast fashion. They communicate the idiosyncrasies of land and species, place and time. The practice of mordanting woven cloth, of exposing fibres to natural tannins or acids to open them in preparation for dyeing, both fixes colour and prevents it fading. An understanding of mordanting – coupled with natural dyes from indigo, madder, rhubarb root, henna, catechu, mulberry, onion skins and cochineal, among countless others – assured the richness and longevity of Indian colours. Unparalleled skills in wax resist and block printing allowed Indian craftspeople to further direct colour application and embellish their creations with intricate

nilaHOUSE, I Heart Nila Sari, 2021

floral patterns and motifs. For these reasons, certain Indian cottons – notably calicoes and *chints* (later chintz) – fuelled a buying frenzy in seventeenth-century Europe.

Although lurid synthetic dyes have long overtaken natural ones in the mass production of global fashion, many Indian designers are taking steps to ensure that the earthy spectrum and nuance of natural dyes remains central to their work. The Sindhi artform of hand blockprinting, known as *ajrakh*, has been in some families for upwards of ten generations. It has recently become a source of renewed appreciation in collaborations between emerging designers and traditional block printers. *Ajrakh* is distinguished by jewel-like colours extracted from natural dyes and by geometric, floral and architectural patterns that seem as strikingly modern today as they were hundreds of years ago. Another designer entirely reconceiving the use of colour is Anavila Misra, whose eponymous label is widely associated with luxurious, understated saris in linen and khadi. Misra works with around 200 weavers based in Phulia, West Bengal, who have come to master the hand-looming of flax, a thread largely foreign to India, creating a whole new class of sari in the process – a sari that is disarmingly casual yet elegant. Her experiments combining zari with linen permit a subtle sheen, while Misra's favoured palette draws directly from the nuanced gradations of the natural world. Other designers are utilising modern dyeing technologies to ensure that quintessentially Indian tones like *gulabi* and *rani* pinks, saffron and mustard yellows, and lush parrot greens are rendered with spectacular depth and fidelity.

Contemporary explorations of both weaving and colour are complemented by an appreciation for the richness and diversity of surface treatments that are currently being revisited and newly created by Indian designers. Like so many aspects of Indian textile production, these reflect India's seemingly inexhaustible capacity to absorb foreign influences and integrate them fruitfully with its own. Gold embroidery has existed in the subcontinent since the Vedic period, around 1500 to 600 BCE. Its usage expanded and was transformed dramatically during the Mughal reign of Akbar, when Persianate zardozi techniques reached peak popularity.

Today, weighty and opulent beading is popular again, found especially in the Indian cities of Lucknow, Hyderabad, Farrukhabad, Chennai and Bhopal. It appears in formal wear and wedding attire across Pakistan and parts of India – so striking that it tends to 'scream' over the quieter, more subtle surface treatments and embroideries favoured in other regions and contexts. These are highlighted by Raw Mango, a design studio and multidisciplinary creative powerhouse founded by Sanjay Garg, whose relationship

Anavila Misra, indigo warp tie-dye linen sari, Santhal Collection, 2015

Ashish Shah, 2017. Anila Sari (left) and Vani Sari (right) wearing Raw Mango, Cloud People collection

with hand-loom began in 2008. The tenderness, softness and intricacy of Chikankari embroidery lies at the centre of a limited run of saris and other garments inspired by the menswear of Awadh and of an accompanying photographic essay entitled 'Cloud People', shot by Ashish Shah.

At the other end of the spectrum – no less flamboyant than traditional zardozi, yet emphatically different in aesthetic and technical execution – is the work of Rimzim Dadu, whose eponymous brand is synonymous with innovative textiles and surfaces. Curiously, Dadu's deconstructing and reconstructing of materials manages to expose the fundamental architecture and composite parts of a sari in entirely fresh ways. Reminiscent of Issey Miyake's bold experiments at the frontiers of East and West, and his success in developing whole new methods of pleating, Dadu's work is at once technical, rigorous and sensual. It defies simple categories and avoids cliché.

There can be no conclusion to any examination of the sari's transformative nature and its continuing appeal. The March 2022 cover of *Vogue India* featured supermodel Lakshmi Menon in an arresting vermillion sari, worn in precolonial fashion with no blouse or undergarments. The cotton sari is by Fabindia, India's best-known clothing retailer and one that supports upwards of 50,000 artisans across the country.[4] It differs only in colour from the saris my mother wore at college. Undeniably, the extraordinary skill of Indian craftspeople, the visionary imaginings of new designers and the devoted patronage of sari enthusiasts everywhere are creating new futures not only for the sari, but also for fashion and textile production globally. In the words of Bandana Tewari, 'When we wrap the length and breadth of a sari, the mindfulness with which we walk and sit evokes a deep self-awareness that is the structure of stillness. This Indian dress is in itself a meditation'.[5] There could hardly be a more powerful response to the ecological violence of fast fashion than this.

1   See Bernard S. Cohn's *Colonialism and Its Forms of Knowledge: The British in India* (Princeton, NJ: Princeton University Press, 1996) on the codification of Indian society during the British colonial period and the resulting construction and reification of social categories.

2   Border&Fall, 'David Abraham & Rakesh Thakore', www.borderandfall.com/abraham-thakore [Accessed 15 January 2023]

3   UN Alliance for Sustainable Fashion, 'Fashion and Sustainable Development', https://unfashionalliance.org [Accessed 6 January 2023]

4   Soutik Biswas, 'Fabindia: Why India's popular clothing brand irks the right-wing', BBC News (25 April 2022), www.bbc.com/news/world-asia-india-61153621 [Accessed 25 January 2023]

5   Bandana Tewari, 'The Sari Holds Our Secrets', *Vogue India* (7 March 2022), www.vogue.in/fashion/content/the-sari-holds-our-secrets [Accessed 3 January 2023]

Asha
Sarabhai

In conversation with Sunil Khilnani

In 1975, Asha Sarabhai established Raag, a studio that was acclaimed for its contemporary interpretations of established Indian processes, including ikat weaving, *kantha* stitching and vegetable dyeing. A pioneering textile designer, her work has proved popular among her contemporaries and was championed by artists such as Robert Rauschenberg, who regularly visited her family residence in Ahmedabad, Gujarat, and modelled her designs.

Known for her handmade, high-quality and uncomplicated approach to textiles, Sarabhai was one of the first Indian designers to gain global recognition – leading to a number of rich collaborations. In 1984, she was invited to launch a label under Miyake Design Studio and later, with Maureen Doherty, opened Egg, a boutique store in London underpinned by Sarabhai's ethos that garments should provide comfort and have longevity. This extended conversation with Sunil Khilnani – author of *The Idea of India* and professor of Politics and History at Ashoka University, India – reflects on her long career in the industry, the legacy of the Weavers' Service Centres and the issue of sustainability.

OVERLEAF   Henri Cartier-Bresson, *Women spreading out their saris before the sun*, Gujarat, 1966

SUNIL KHILNANI   The sari has an incredibly rich history of creative and productive skills: weaving, dyeing, printing, embellishing. Embodied in these techniques is a connection to handicraft that hasn't survived easily in the age of modern industrial and consumer capitalism. Sari making has needed support, particularly its more refined and labour-intensive forms. How has the lesser-known history of sari making been kept alive in India in this period of industrial production and mass consumption?

ASHA SARABHAI   There have been a lot of imports – first from Japan, now from China – of industrially produced saris, which mimic the visual designs of old saris, largely in synthetic fabrics: nylons, chiffons. Now Indian textile mills also pour out these fabrics, which has affected the social ecologies of production and use in all sorts of ways. For instance, the adoption of new industrially woven saris has edged out the local *dhobi* system, the laundrymen and -women who used to collect, wash and iron saris. The new fabrics are wash 'n' wear – practical for working women, but perhaps not ideal fabrics for the Indian climate. That iconic Henri Cartier-Bresson image of saris being dried on the beds of the Sabarmati River in Ahmedabad, not far from Gandhi Ashram – that's not something you would see now.

Sidney B. Felsen, Robert Rauschenberg and Asha Sarabhai, Ahmedabad, Gujarat, 1975

SK   Your own engagement with the design and making of textiles dates back to the mid-1970s, and to the Vishwa-karma projects and exhibitions of the 1980s. Could you talk a bit about the historical background, the interventions that allowed weavers and producers of hand-loomed saris to stay afloat during the 1950s and 1960s?

AS   The Weavers' Service Centres, which were established by the government, were crucial, especially for the handwoven-sari industry – as opposed to what's called the power-loom sector, which was widely adopted in the post-independence decades. Some of the more enlightened among India's elite – including Indira Gandhi herself, who was a great wearer and connoisseur of saris, and her close associate Pupul Jayakar – became worried by the demise of the hand loom. They feared the destruction not just of everything that went with that aesthetic – that quality of design, of structure, of weaving, tactility – but also the livelihoods of many millions. I think quite a few people realised the problems the hand-loom sector was facing, and they set up support facilities, which could help with technical issues of production, but also with design input.

SK   So, at that point, the Planning Commission took
the initiative at a governmental level to establish regional
Weavers' Service Centres across India?

AS   Yes, absolutely. It started initially with three or four,
then grew to a network of around twenty-five centres
across the country. They ran different programmes for skills
training and technical work and sample developments, and
later began to work closely with institutions like the National
Institute of Fashion Technology (NIFT), which was set up in
the mid-1980s. The aim here was to make products relevant
to an urban audience as well, and to try to keep the industry
alive by connecting it to contemporary tastes and uses.
There was a cost factor involved, since the market was
being flooded with cheaper alternatives to hand-loom
fabrics. So large swathes of people who couldn't afford
a hand-loom sari were buying alternatives. The Weavers'
Service Centres were dedicated to resolving problems of
sourcing yarn, of dyeing, of technical issues in weaving and
of trying to make the process more cost-effective. They were
regional, and each region had different strengths and raw
materials: the cotton from Andhra [Pradesh], for instance,
was very different from Bihar – so the material itself varied,
from the basic yarn upwards. So they were really critical.

SK   That attention to production as well as design is worth
noting. On the one hand, they were harking back to a deep
theme in nineteenth- and twentieth-century India, picked
up famously by Mahatma Gandhi, about the vital survival
of hand loom and hand craft, which had been destroyed
during the colonial period. But the interest in design also
came from a more contemporary direction. It was Pupul
Jayakar who convinced Indira Gandhi and [Jawaharlal]
Nehru to invite Charles and Ray Eames to write a report,
which became one of the founding documents of modern
design in India and led to the establishment of the National
Institute of Design in Ahmedabad.[1] So the impulse behind
the Weavers' Service Centres might be described as both
Gandhian and modernist in its ambitions ...

PM Dalwadi, 1964. Charles Eames at the National
Institute of Design, Ahmedabad, Gujarat

AS   Indeed.

SK   You worked closely with Martand Singh, or 'Mapu'
as he was known, who was a seminal figure in the revival
of hand skills in textiles. How did that come about?

AS   We met through the wonderful designer Shona Ray,
when Mapu moved from Delhi to Ahmedabad to work at the
Calico Museum of Textiles. Pupul Jayakar and Indira Gandhi

wanted to showcase the immense variety and skill of Indian crafts and textiles, with the hope of creating openings for Indian products in an international market. Pupul knew Mapu well, and asked whether he would be involved in the textile aspect, mainly saris and fabric. By this point, we had become good friends, and he asked if I could be involved too and help develop ideas for it. These Vishwakarma exhibitions showcased on an international stage (at the Commonwealth Institute [now the Design Museum] in London, in Paris and in Frankfurt) the work of India's master weavers.

A crucial thing we agreed on was to move away from a nostalgic revivalist attitude (the 'splendour that was India' kind of thing) and to search for new possibilities for these skills. It wasn't just about remaking heavily brocaded Banarasi saris or intricately figurative Patola ikats from Patan, but rather whether we could figure out a contemporary idiom for them, which would make them '*of* their times'.

The first stop on our journey was Benares, where the Weavers' Service Centre was headed by a wonderful man called Supakar-ji, who knew all the weavers and the possibilities of that region. We looked at many things that were being woven at that point and I noticed something didn't feel or look right with the brocade work. Rather than being embedded in the structure of the sari as it used to be in the past, it sort of stood out – it wasn't fully integrated. As we kept talking with the weavers, one master weaver said, 'You're absolutely right.' He told us about a process at the yarn stage, called *paat bana*, where the yarn was not given a high twist but was drawn, resulting in textures that were flatter and denser – and without a high sheen. We managed to have a few saris, with much less elaborate brocading, made for the exhibition. We were trying to get back to the basic structure of the weave itself, and to use brocade in a more contemporary way yet still working with existing motifs, like the *ambi* or mango pattern, and others that were part of the dictionary of design. With the Patolas from Patan, we moved away from densely patterned saris replete with all sorts of wonderful creatures and a multiplicity of colours, trying out three geometric patterns in three single colours instead. So it was that kind of intervention: unearthing the original technique, which opened up contemporary possibilities.

SK   The work that you did in the 1980s, and into the 1990s – did it establish a benchmark for the best that can be done with different techniques and weaving forms?

AS   I think there was a shared desire to create benchmarks to show what was still possible. We worked very closely with the Weavers' Service Centres and the artists within them to see whether the 'splendour that was Indian textiles' could still be made – with a difference – in the 1980s, or whether those skills had disappeared altogether. Thankfully, they hadn't. This whole repertoire of different regional production and skills still existed. Whether it was Paithanis from Maharashtra or the Patolas, or the Kanjeeverams and Venkatgiris from south India, all these things were still possible, if given support – which in this case came from the government.

SK   The work done under the auspices of the Vishwakarma exhibitions, and your collaboration with Issey Miyake, were internationally recognised in France by the Musée des Arts Décoratifs and in London by the V&A and its Boilerhouse Project. Your own projects also became part of the V&A collection. But that didn't necessarily create a market for such work in India – except perhaps among a minuscule, rarefied clientele. What was missing, and why has it begun only recently to resonate?

AS   I think a lot of the people who had the wherewithal to buy things like that within India were more interested in buying designer brands from abroad. There was plenty of more elaborate stuff, which had busy markets within India. But people had moved away from the elegant simplicity of the south Indian, or Keralan, saris – just the unbleached off-white with the bands of gold zari.

SK   You might think of it as a more purist idiom, rather than a simple one.

AS   Well, it was purist or, as I mean it, simple in the best sense: a kind of clarity, of form and design, arrived at through the elimination of the redundant and the distracting. And it was perhaps only when the work began to be recognised further afield – when Issey Miyake began selling the things we were making at Raag's workshops and a little later when, after my *Contemporary Tradition* exhibition at the V&A, Maureen Doherty and I opened Egg in London – that people in India began to engage with the work. And even then that was a very small group of people. Costs were part of it, since many of these experiments were only within the reach of a financially endowed group who at that point weren't that interested.
    When, years ago, I first started working with textiles and making things, the hope was to introduce a new idiom within Indian 'making'. But when I went to government enterprises like the Central Cottage Industries Emporium or to the Handicraft and Handlooms Exports Corporation (HHEC), they kept saying things like, 'if you cut out that workmanship, and if you take away that, and if you don't do the hand stitching, then we maybe can market it and it will be viable commer-

cially'. Unfortunately, that missed my point completely, which was to make things that looked, felt and lasted well, so one consumed less and enjoyed better!

SK   You mention the issue of sustainability. What are your views on that – not just economic sustainability, but more generally?

AS   I think there is an ethical stance to it, as well. For example, not so long ago, there was this huge coverage of Lakmé Fashion Week in the Indian press about designers using organic cotton and about sustainability. And everyone felt very excited and sort of virtuous about it. Yet, at the same time, there were cotton farmers who were committing suicide in the South because they couldn't sustain their lives or livelihoods. That's something we cannot afford to ignore but need to highlight, to examine and to reflect on carefully. There are a lot of wonderful designers, who've done great one-offs – or two or three offs – of saris. But, sadly, this isn't enough to sustain a whole industry of making, living and doing. R̥ta Kapur Chishti, for instance, has done amazing things with real khadi, but that kind of dedicated work is very small in comparison to the larger picture of what India needs.

The immediate problems with India are really clear: there's a need for food, shelter and the distribution of resources. And these issues are still very much in need of urgent address. If we can find ways to get design and designers involved in this way, I think there's a much larger role to be played. Something like the authenticity of organic cotton is often made the issue but, far more importantly, is the farmer able to ensure that, given the minuscule returns they get for it – a very base, basic price – it's a viable *livelihood*? I'm afraid at present 'the Empire of Cotton' still rules!

1   This was The India Report of 1958, which suggested that India's 'immediate problems are well defined: FOOD, SHELTER, DISTRIBUTION, POPULATION.'

Abraham
& Thakore

David Abraham interviewed by Debika Ray

David Abraham and Rakesh Thakore established their acclaimed fashion house in 1992. They had met as students at the National Institute of Design in Ahmedabad, where they underwent rigorous training in Indian textile craft but grounded in a modernist language. Together, they formed a design studio whose first collection of accessories was bought by both The Conran Shop in London and Browns in New York, and yet whose fashionable styles stay true to their origins in traditional Indian crafts and hand-loomed textiles.

Crisp, clean and minimalist, Abraham & Thakore's work is highly respected by craft experts and design practitioners alike. It is characterised by a progressive approach to hand loom, with cuts and motifs that are conventionally found in the context of tailoring. Abraham & Thakore's collaborations with craft clusters in West Bengal, Gujarat and Andhra Pradesh demonstrate their sustained commitment to nurturing regional textile heritage, which they have successfully adapted for the contemporary consumer. Abraham is interviewed here by Debika Ray, editor of *Crafts* magazine, about the roots of their brand and the future of their business, which has recently expanded to encompass homeware and men's collections.

RIGHT   Abraham & Thakore, Embroidered Silk × Cotton Sari, 2019
OVERLEAF   Manou, 2017. Lakshmi Rana wearing sari by Abraham & Thakore, backstage at Delhi Fashion Week

DEBIKA RAY Let's start by talking about your creative origins. Could you tell me about your time studying textile design at the National Institute of Design (NID) in Ahmedabad in the 1980s?

DAVID ABRAHAM The NID was extremely formative for me. At the time, design was a relatively new phenomenon in India, and our faculty was starting to look at craft and textiles around us as a source of inspiration and a means to develop its own design language. The institute is located in the state of Gujarat, an area that's rich with craft, so we studied different weavers and printers around us and we also had access to an incredible repository of traditional Indian textiles. The programme was very hands-on – the first thing a student is given is their own loom, and we were taught how to weave, print and dye fabrics. What I tried to do later was completely different, but these experiences provided me with the basis for my practice as a designer, and I continue to draw on that now.

DR How did you go on to develop your own design language, particularly for the sari?

DA After graduating, I worked in Delhi for a company based in New York on ready-to-wear garments for the American market, which meant I was exposed to a completely different understanding of fashion. For the first ten years of our own business, we were mostly selling in London – so I was still designing products for the international market. At the time, this didn't include clothing from outside the Western construct of

fashion – anything else was seen as 'costume'. Fashion was controlled by Western gatekeepers, which I found to be problematic.

These experiences made me question fashion in the Indian context, and when we first presented a collection during a fashion show in Delhi in 2010, we tried to address these issues. Around that time, international fashion brands were starting to permeate India. Their clothing represented modernity and a move away from tradition and, for a lot of young women, an expression of their

independence and identity. But there was a contrast between the clothes that were being imported and what people were actually wearing: they would adapt these garments for the Indian context – for example, a short dress would be worn with trousers, like a kurta.

We felt that – for this younger, fashion-conscious customer – the sari was beginning to seem dated, so for our first collection we decided to deconstruct it. We made it a metre shorter – four-and-a-half, rather than five-and-a-half metres – to cut the amount of fabric around the waist. We

tied it shorter, cropped around the ankle. We changed the proportions, by adding heavy platform clogs and belts to create more defined silhouettes without stitching. And, instead of the traditional choli, we added things like shirts and jackets to create a very designed look. We also played with motifs. One black sari – which was acquired by the V&A – was embroidered with fine traditional *jamdani* embroidery but featured motifs inspired by election symbols, which are universal in India. Every season we still do a sari – some are slightly constructed, some partially stitched, some with zip-up sides. We've tried different ways of making it easier to wear.

DR With the X-ray Sari – one of your garments in the exhibition – you used an unexpected palette of materials. What was the thinking behind this design?

DA That sari was part of a collection we made out of recycled, post-consumer waste, with a company that produces fabrics from plastic water bottles. The sari is made from this yarn and ornamented with sequins cut from discarded hospital X-rays. The blouse has a running-stitch pattern printed on it as a reference to *kantha*, one of the traditional techniques of India, which involves layering together recycled fabrics. It's all about repurposing old materials.

DR Another sari in the Design Museum show is the Herringbone Georgette Sari, which explores form as well as material. Could you tell me about that?

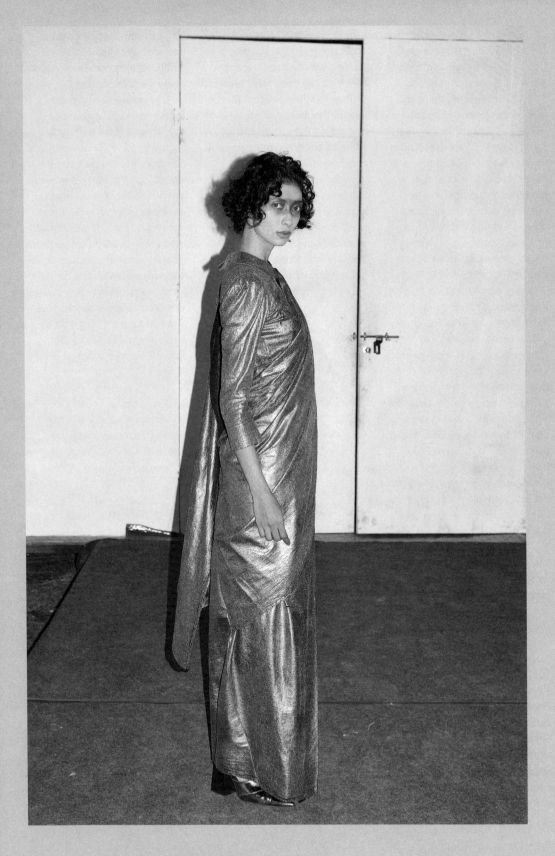

THE OFFBEAT SARI

DA   It came from a collection that was exploring traditional menswear: the shapes of men's clothing as well as fabrics traditionally used for men's suits, such as tweed and herringbone. We wanted to translate these textiles into something appropriate for womenswear: the herringbone pattern was block printed on to georgette fabric, which meant that a thick, heavy cloth was translated into something light and sheer. We teamed that with a shirt on which the block printing was done once it was stitched, which makes the pattern really patchy – here, the technique and the construction are in dialogue with one another.

DR   Another traditional textile you've long worked with is khadi. What were you trying to do with that when you created the Laminated Gold Khadi Sari?

DA   Khadi is always associated with something that's quite serious, earnest and full of good intentions, as well as having political undertones. We wanted to have a little fun with it, so we laminated it with gold foil, which is the most opposite association we could think of. Initially it looked a bit too shiny, which wasn't quite the mood we wanted, so we washed and distressed it – then created a sari and blouse with that fabric. The distressing was done by hand and really brings the texture of the material out through the lamination.

DR   The Leaf Ikat Sari is much more of a classic design. What were you trying to explore there?

DA   Yes, it's a full five-and-a-half metres, with a very fine gold border. We often take a particular form – in this case, a leaf – and work with it using different techniques to see what happens when the materials and methods change, and when different craftspeople interact with it. For this sari, ikat weavers blew up the leaf to an enormous size and placed it on the pallu – with the rest of the sari remaining plain. Ikat normally incorporates a repeated pattern because of the technique, which involves tying and dyeing all the threads, so here they were breaking those rules. It took the weavers a long time to figure that out but, after four months, this piece appeared.

DR   How does your relationship with craftspeople contribute to the design process?

DA   The sari is the most important garment in India in many ways, and some of the greatest work in Indian textile craft has been developed specifically for it. Structures are developed based on the way in which the fabric wraps around the body: the border, the pallu and the motifs are all designed to fall in a particular place. We believe that process informs the design – it dictates the shape, the form, the colours that you use. And it's not just craft: we do a lot of digital printing and work with technical fabrics – even in those cases, the material informs the direction.
   I think this is especially true for a lot of Indian fashion designers because, unlike many other parts of the world, we have a large living tradition of textiles that is very accessible and inexpensive to work with. Every aspect of Indian society has a very strong relationship to textiles, which is quite special.

DR   Who are your saris for?

DA   They're for people who wear all types of clothing. I don't think we're talking to the traditional sari wearer – we're talking to a customer who is as comfortable wearing a tailored suit in the day as a sari in the evening. For many people, the sari has become a garment for occasional dressing, rather than regular wear – part of a composite wardrobe. In India now there is much more awareness of how it's necessary for us to find a language that is relevant to us, while still being international.

DR   What is next for you as a brand and business?

DA   We've had investment from a very large company, which means we are in the process of expanding and opening more stores. Making on a larger scale is something we're in the process of figuring out with our craftspeople, who often work slowly and in small quantities. It's challenging but also interesting, both for us and for them. It's also important because, for craftspeople, this is a way of growing the market for higher-priced products.
   Fortunately, Indian textile craft is still alive and kicking. With shifts like this and the efforts of many other Indian designers, I foresee it remaining strong. There was a time when everyone was saying 'it has died' – but it certainly doesn't look that way to me!

THIS SPREAD   Sunil Kumar for Dastkari Haat Samiti and Google Arts & Culture, 2018. The process of
                making a Banarasi brocade, Benares

ABOVE + TOP   HolyWeaves, Benares, 2022. Weaver on a hand loom

HolyWeaves, Benares, 2022. Hand-loom workshop

Botanical extract of *indigofera tinctoria* or
indigo cake at KMA Exports, one of the oldest
indigo-producing families in south India, 2018

Briana Blasko, *Indigo Extraction 4, Tamil Nadu*, 2010

Tamarind indigo vats at nilaHOUSE, Jaipur, 2022

ABOVE   Prarthna Singh, 2019. Indigo dye vat,
         nilaHOUSE, Jaipur
OVERLEAF Briana Blasko, *Indigo Extraction 3,*
         Tamil Nadu, 2010

NILA
     HOUSE
Art and science – almost alchemy and magic – are used to create
this extraordinary colour: indigo, or *neel*. To extract the dye, the indigo
plant is grown, harvested and fermented through a complex process.
nilaHOUSE is a non-profit organisation reviving natural indigo and
sustainable livelihoods by collaborating with farmers, craftspeople
and designers. This process depicts yarn being dyed three times to
give the sari a depth of colour.

THE OFFBEAT SARI

ABOVE + BOTTOM RIGHT   Flo Hanatschek, 2019. Dyes used by Sufiyan Khatri during the block-printing process, Ajrakhpur, Kutch, Gujarat

Display of natural dyes used by Sufiyan Khatri, Gujarat, 2019

THIS SPREAD   Flo Hanatschek, 2019. Hand-carved wood blocks used for block printing
by Sufiyan Khatri at his studio in Ajrakhpur, Kutch, Gujarat

ABOVE   Sufiyan Khatri block printing at his studio
RIGHT   Block-printed textiles by Sufiyan Khatri
OVERLEAF   Flo Hanatschek, 2019. Printed saris by Sufiyan
Khatri drying in the sun

SUFIYAN
ISMAIL KHATRI

Ajrakh is an ancient method of block printing that traditionally
comprises motifs based on Islamic geometry. Designer–artisan
Sufiyan Ismail Khatri – a ninth-generation block printer – reinterprets
the language of *ajrakh* through contemporary design. These saris
are designed using many hand-carved wood blocks and undergo a
complex process of printing and dyeing using natural pigments and
natural resists.

ABOVE + TOP   VegNonVeg, Ajrakh Camo Sari, 2022. Printed by Sufiyan Khatri
LEFT   Abraham & Thakore, IKAT Sari, 2023

ABOVE   Weaver at the Paiwand Studio, Noida, Uttar Pradesh, 2022
RIGHT   Paiwand × Naina Jain, hand-woven Upcycled Bandhani Sari, 2022

Paiwand, hand-woven upcycled fabric, 2022

Ekaya (Revival Project), hand-woven Zari Red Silk Sari, 2021

Ekaya (Revival Project), hand-woven Green Zari Silk Sari, 2021

Ekaya (Revival Project), hand-woven
Yellow Zari Tissue Sari, 2021

ABOVE   nilaHOUSE, khadi weaver, Kaladera, Rajasthan, 2018
BELOW   Prarthna Singh, 2020. WomenWeave, hand-spun cotton yarn on a loom, Maheshwar, Madhya Pradesh

Abraham & Thakore, Gold Khadi Sari, 2016

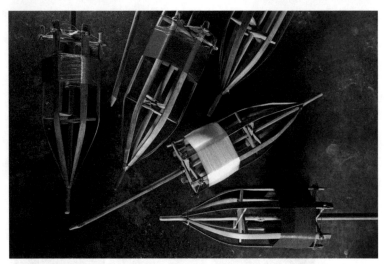

ABOVE   Advaya, The House of Angadi, 2019. Spindles of silk yarn used in the creation of
            Kanjeevaram saris, Kanchipuram, Tamil Nadu
BELOW   Advaya, The House of Angadi, 2019. Weavers holding up punch cards used in
            the creation of Kanjeevaram saris, Kanchipuram, Tamil Nadu

Advaya, The House of Angadi, 2019. The ritual 'drawing of ends', is the process of weaving in the threads of a fresh warp as it is draped across the loom

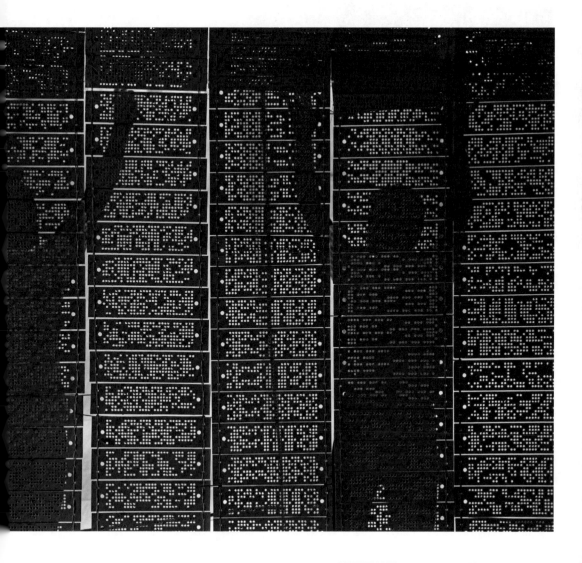

Advaya, The House of Angadi, The Molten Sky, Kanjeevaram pure silk and real zari tissue sari, made with *khadua* technique, The Eternal Series collection, 2021

ABOVE   Advaya, The House of Angadi, The Princess-Pink, Kanjeevaram pure silk and real zari sari, The Eternal Series collection, 2021

OVERLEAF   Advaya, The House of Angadi, 2019. The process of street warping, performed in the mornings, is a common sight in weaving clusters across India

Munsif Molu, 2018. Elizabeth Mech Boro wearing sculpted metallic sari by Rimzim Dadu

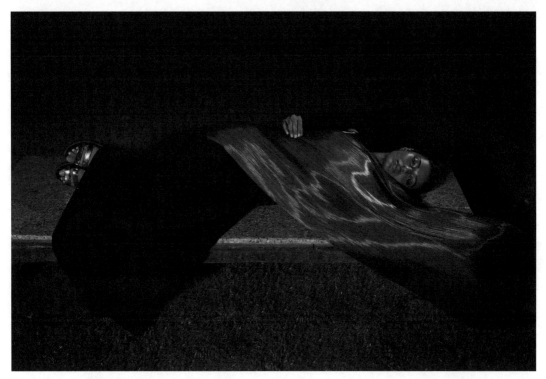

Rimzim Dadu, Steel Wire Sari, 2016

ABOVE   Raw Mango, Mahejabi Chikankari Sari, Cloud People collection, 2017
OPPOSITE   Raw Mango, Faidah Sari, Cloud People collection, 2017

Raw Mango, Darkshan Sari, Cloud People collection, 2017

Afterword

Priya Khanchandani

On Friday 7 November 2014, the then newly appointed prime minister Narendra Modi visited Benares, where he laid the foundation stone of a new Trade Facilitation Centre and Crafts Museum, launching a broader government project to revive hand-loom weaving with Benares at its heart.[1] At a podium decorated with orange and yellow flowers, Modi referred to the idea that every mother in India wished to give her daughter a Banarasi sari as a wedding present, and explained, 'textile workers weave not just cloth, but the fabric of a cohesive, harmonious society.'[2] His words drew on the emotional appeal of textiles and connected hand-loom cloth with the fabric of India's national identity.

Benares is by no means the only city in India with a rich history of hand-loom weaving, but it is the oldest city in India – and, hence, a place synonymous with India's heritage. It is also a particularly auspicious site for Hindus. Located on the left bank of the Ganga, the holy river where Hindus undergo ritual purification, it is packed with shrines and temples, and visibly transformed by the Hindu festivals that are celebrated there – including the Ganga festival dedicated to the goddess of the river, when thousands of lamps are set afloat.

The policies concerning the revival project occupied more than 100 pages of the Ministry of Textiles' Annual Report 2015–16. They covered investment in equipment used by weavers; the provision of social welfare, insurance and marketing; and opportunities to upskill the sector, all at a national level.[3] One scheme provided subsidised loans and credit cards to weavers to enable them to multiply their scale of production and grow their business. Another created access to expos, events, craft fairs and other retail sites, even proposing an e-marketing platform formed in conjunction with online retailer Flipkart. The initiatives specific to Benares included setting up several facility centres, each with a yarn depot, office, internet and

Lantern festival by the Ganges River, Benares

equipment for winding, warping and dyeing thread before it is woven, as well as full-time and technically qualified staff.

The government's commitment to developing the local hand-loom sector has been both concerted and dedicated. While it continues to promote craft practice in a genuine fashion, the cultural context of hand-loom fabric in India makes the state's revival project an unequivocally politicised act, aligning the Bharatiya Janata Party (BJP) with the patriotism often associated with hand-loom cloth in ways that also reposition it to sit with their right-wing, pro-Hindu agenda. During the independence movement, cloth became closely linked with the revival of Indian nationalism in a way that constituted an act of resistance, underpinned by the quest for self-determination in the face of colonial rule. The domestic production of khadi was mobilised against the monopolistic import of British-made cloth that had resulted in the almost total destruction of the hand-loom industry, galvanising a revolutionary movement propelled by the principles of self-sufficiency. Today, the promotion of hand-loom cloth by the BJP associates the party with aspects of Gandhian nationalism that conceived of India as a proudly craft-based nation. In reality, the BJP's form of exclusionary nationalism is entirely different – based on pro-Hindu policies to the detriment of other religious sects and ethnic minorities, in particular Muslims, and embedded in a wider drive to boost India's commercial prospects to foreign investors through globally oriented policies such as 'Make in India'.

On the surface, the hand-loom revival adds a nuanced dimension to 'Make in India' by implying that its project is about more than just accruing wealth, imbuing it with concern for an aspect of Indian culture that is considered integral to national identity. However, the BJP has also been heavily criticised for revitalising ethno-nationalism – despite India having been founded as a secular state – and for empowering right-wing Hindu extremism that has caused public unrest and led to riots.[4] In this context, the choice of Benares as the centre of the textile-revival project cannot be read as politically neutral.

The progressive nature of the contemporary sari – both its innovation and capacity to absorb new ideas – is a shining light amid an increasingly entrenched backdrop of conservatism that has profoundly shaken the roots of liberal thinking in India over the past decade. Its flourishing, particularly through new approaches to hand-loom weaving, might have been indicative of a broader cultural renaissance, one extending beyond the remit of the sari. But in fact, since independence was attained in 1947, Indian democracy has never been under such threat as it is today – its arts, media and courts all find themselves under incremental pressure to align with the BJP's controversial policies and ideological positions. The sanctioned destruction of a sixteenth-century mosque in the town of Ayodhya on the grounds that the land once hosted a temple, the exclusion of Muslims from a new Act providing sanctuary to people from three neighbouring countries fleeing religious persecution, and the formation of Hindu nationalist gangs who lynch Muslims on suspicion of eating beef (the cow is considered sacred to Hindus) – all are examples of how Indian culture is at the behest of a frightening political reality.

There are divided views as to where the sari falls within this context. At one extreme, some have argued that Modi's appropriation of hand-loom textiles has attempted to turn the sari into a weapon for a BJP version of Indian nationalism; others argue that the sari was always ideological, and whether the BJP or their political opponents, the Congress Party, are incumbent, it will always be equated with Indian identity. Either way, there are strong opinions among commentators and sari evangelists alike as to whether the garment is a symbol for politics or whether it is beyond politics altogether. Despite the complex history specific to hand-loom cloth, I would like to think that the sari transcends Indian politics – after all, it does not belong to India alone, but also to other regions of South Asia which were once indistinguishable by national border, notably Bangladesh, Pakistan, Sri Lanka and Nepal. Still, there are hints of attempts to fetter the sari's freedom which, in the context of the BJP's broader conservative agenda, shouldn't escape our notice. For example, Modi's remarks that the commonly found Nivi sari drape originated in Gujarat, a predominantly Hindu state, suggest that the progressiveness of the sari is not protected from being reinterpreted according to the BJP's revisionist Hindutva perspective.[5] (In actual fact, the Nivi drape derives from the Parsi drape, fused with the Bengali style, as interpreted by Jnanadanandini Tagore during her time in Bombay – now Mumbai). Elsewhere, there has been outcry among far-right Hindu trolls against Bollywood star Deepika Padukone for wearing a saffron-coloured bikini (while dancing to a song titled 'Besharam Rang', meaning 'shameless colour') in the film *Pathaan* (2023), on the grounds that saffron is the sacred hue of their religion – yet another sign that fashion is no longer protected from censure.

In a January 2023 lecture at the India International Centre in New Delhi, historian Romila Thapar critiqued the way in which history is increasingly being reread through this nationalist lens. She warned that the notion of India as a single, unitary nation was being threatened by the government, which misinterprets the past as having created two distinctly different forms of nationhood: Hinduism and Islam.[6] Every attempt has been made to read the sari as a cultural object through this book, and the exhibition that it accompanies, but, in light of the revisionist tendencies that Thapar highlights, it would be remiss not to contextualise it within the current political landscape. We must acknowledge that – however secular, free and progressive the contemporary sari may be – it does not exist in a vacuum.

Despite broad attempts to impose cultural conservatism – as well as the political messaging around hand-loom cloth – the sari has, perhaps surprisingly, largely resisted censure, managing to survive as a symbol of fresh perspectives. Those who wear the garment as an assertion of Indian identity today are, in fact, often violently anti-BJP, self-professed sari progressives. The sari has also demonstrated its ability to act as a leveller across social divides and to communicate through a language of pattern, weave and motifs – formed through ingenuity on the part of both designers and wearers – that transcends politics. Within the pages of this book, we have seen some of the richly creative ways in which the contemporary sari embodies memory, ideology and empowerment – reflecting a spectrum of identities, including emergent voices who were not previously active in mainstream society. Wearers in India, the world's largest democracy, and people across the rest of the sari-wearing world, including the diaspora, have individualised it, enabling it to shapeshift and flourish in a way that celebrates the diversity of the society it serves. May they continue to reimagine the sari far into the future.

1   'Akhilesh Yadav to welcome Narendra Modi in Varanasi', *Times of India* (7 November 2014), www.timesofindia.indiatimes.com/india/akhilesh-yadav-to-welcome-narendra-modi-in-varanasi/articleshow/45064525.cms [Accessed 14 February 2023]

2   Government of India, 'Press Information Bureau: Prime Minister's Office', 7 November 2014, www.pib.gov.in/newsite/PrintRelease.aspx?relid=111150 [Accessed 12 February]

3   Government of India, *Annual Report of the Ministry of Textiles 2015–2016*, www.texmin.nic.in [Accessed 16 February 2023]

4   Enacted in 1976, the Preamble to the Constitution asserts that India is a secular nation.

5   'PM Modi reveals who started the tradition of draping saree with "ulta pallu"', *Times of India* (24 December 2020), www.timesofindia.indiatimes.com/india/pm-modi-reveals-who-started-the-tradition-of-draping-saree-with-ulta-pallu/articleshow/79941737.cms [Accessed 15 February 2023]

6   Romila Thapar, 'Our History, Their History, Whose History?', C.D. Deshmukh Memorial Lecture 2023, India International Centre (14 January 2023), www.iicdelhi.in/programmes/dr-cd-deshmukh-memorial-lecture-2023 [Accessed 16 February 2023]

OVERLEAF   NORBLACK NORWHITE, hand-painted chiffon saris, Holidaze collection, 2020

Index

Illustrations and captions are denoted by the use of *italic* page numbers.

Biographies

Abraham & Thakore
is one of India's most successful and respected design resources for fashion, accessories and textile products for the home.

Pragya Agarwal
is an author, a behavioural and data scientist, a professor of Social Inequities and Injustice, and the founder of research think tank The 50 Percent.

Amit Aggarwal
is a Delhi-based couture house widely renowned for its craftsmanship-first approach and for sourcing sustainable materials.

Dal Chodha
is a London-based writer and editor-in-chief of *Archivist Addendum*. He is currently stage one leader of the BA Fashion Communication & Promotion course at Central Saint Martins.

Sonia Faleiro
is the author of *The Good Girls: An Ordinary Killing*. She is also the programme director of the literary incubator South Asia Speaks and the co-founder of Deca.

Phyllida Jay
is an independent fashion researcher whose work explores fashion, craft and design.

Priya Khanchandani
is Head of Curatorial at the Design Museum, and the lead curator and editor of *The Offbeat Sari* exhibition and book.

Sunil Khilnani
is a scholar of social and political sciences, writer of Indian histories, and is currently a professor of Political Science and History at Ashoka University, India.

Anupama Kundoo
is currently a professor at Potsdam School of Architecture, Germany, and the head of urban design, Auroville.

Aanchal Malhotra
is co-founder of the Museum of Material Memory, and the author of *Remnants of Partition* and *In the Language of Remembering*.

Tara Mayer
is a cultural historian of South Asia and an associate professor of Teaching in the Institute for Gender, Race, Sexuality and Social Justice at the University of British Columbia.

Sabyasachi Mukherjee
is the founder and CEO of Sabyasachi, a leading Indian fashion design house bringing together craft with a contemporary bridal client-base.

NORBLACK NORWHITE
is a design house and cultural platform inspired by handcrafted Indian textiles, committed to reinterpreting the stereotypes around a contemporary India.

Debika Ray
is the editor of *Crafts* as well as head of editorial at the UK Crafts Council.

Asha Sarabhai
is a textile designer and the founder of Gujarat-based design studio Raag.

Amardeep Singh Dhillon
is a journalist and bartender based in London. Their writing has been published in various outlets including the *Independent*, *Vice*, the *i paper* and Novara Media.

Himanshu Verma
is an art curator and the founder of Red Earth. He is also the founder of The Saree Festival.

Picture Credits

Every reasonable attempt has been made to identify owners of copyright. Errors and omissions notified to the publisher will be corrected in subsequent editions.

Abbreviations are: t – top, b – bottom

A: Advaya, The House of Angadi. Photo Chirodeep Chaudhuri: pp.182, 183, 186–187; Advaya, The House of Angadi. Photo Rid Burman: pp.184, 185; AKAARO. Photo Shivam Pathak: p.22; AKAARO. Photo Aakanksha Arun: p.35; AKAARO. Photo Hansraj Dochaniya: p.36b; Colour palette by AKAARO. Photo Natalia Davidovich/Adobe Stock: p.36t; Amit Aggarwal. Photo Arun Sharma: p.65; Amit Aggarwal. Photo Pranoy Sarkar: pp.66, 68, 69; Anavila Misra. Photo Shivam Misra: p.146; Photo Anupam Nath: p.136; Photo AP/Shutterstock: p.137; Courtesy of Architectural Digest, Condé Nast, India. Photo Rema Chaudary: p.110; Courtesy of the artist and Perrotin. Photo Claire Dorn: p.75; ASHDEEN: p.41; ASHDEEN. Photo Hormis Antony Tharakan: p.40 B: Courtesy of Bodice: p.39; Courtesy of Bodice. Photo Avishkar Jadon: pp.13, 38; Courtesy of Border&Fall. © The Sari Series: pp.59, 78, 79; Photo © Briana Blasko: pp.164b, 166–167 C: Photo Chantal Garcia: p.92; The Cleveland Museum of Art. Gift of The Textile Arts Club 1981.218: p.144 D: Courtesy Dastkari Haat Samiti and Google Arts & Culture. Photo Sunil Kumar: pp.160, 161; Photo © David Mansell/reportdigital.co.uk: p.116; © Diksha Khanna Design Studio: p.25; Photo Dinodia Photos/Alamy Stock Photo: pp.117t, 127, 129t E: Ekaya. Photo Prerna Nainwal (@prernanainwal). Stylist James Lalthanzuala (@jameslalthanzuala): pp.2, 178, 179; Ekaya × Masaba. Photo Bikramjit Bose: pp.132, 133; Photo courtesy The Estate of Amrita Sher-Gil: p.18 F: Photo © Flo Andrea Hanatschek: pp.168, 169b, 170t, 171, 172–173 H: © Henri Cartier-Bresson © Fondation Henri Cartier-Bresson/Magnum Photos: pp.150–151; Photo Heritage Image Partnership Ltd/Alamy Stock Photo. © Museum of London/Heritage-Images: p.126; Courtesy of Himanshu Verma. Photo Kiran Multani: p.97; Courtesy of Himanshu Verma. Photo Parikhit Pal: p.99; Courtesy of HolyWeaves, holyweaves.com. Photo Umang Agrawal: pp.162, 163; HUEMN. Photo Pankaj Dahalia. Talent Rittika Ray. Stylist Aayushi Ratan. Makeup artist Sanya Dhingra: pp.27, 43; HUEMN. Photo Pankaj Dahalia. Talent Rachi Chitkara: p.42b; HUEMN. Talent Maansi (@mmmaansi). Styling Aayushi Ratan (@_floo_powder) and Divya Beniwal (@divyabeniwal): p.42t I: Imperial War Museums. Ministry of Information Second World War Official Collection. © IWM IB 698: p.16; Courtesy of India Hobson/Vogue/Condé Nast. Photo India Hobson:

Courtesy of Irene Yee and Prerna Dangi. Photo Irene Yee. Wardrobe Satya Paul: pp.82–83 J: Photo Joerg Boethling/Alamy Stock Photo: pp.117b, 119, 139b; Photo John Henry Claude Wilson/robertharding/Alamy Stock Photo: p.192; The J. Paul Getty Museum, Los Angeles. Photo Shepherd & Robertson: p.90 K: Courtesy of Kallol Datta. Photo Siddhartha Hajra: pp.70, 71; Courtesy of Kallol Datta. Photo Parak Sarungbam: p.73; L: Little Shilpa. Photo Prasad Naik: p.94 M: Courtesy of Mamta Sharma Das. Photo Saurabh Dasgupta: p.106b; Photo Manou/Wearabout blog (@wearaboutblog): pp.37, 106t, 158; Photo Mansell Collection/The LIFE Picture Collection/Shutterstock: p.128; Photo Margaret Bourke-White/The LIFE Picture Collection/Shutterstock: p.129b; Courtesy of Mithu Sen and Abdullah Usman Khan. Photo Abdullah Usman Khan: p.107; Photo Munsif Molu. Stylist Chandni Bahri. Hair and makeup Flavia Giuliodori. Talent Elizabeth Mech Boro of Anima Creatives Mumbai: pp.34, 188, 208; Courtesy of Museum of Art and Photography (MAP): p.17 N: Courtesy of Natasha Poonawalla. Photo Greg Swales (@gregswalesart). Bustier encircled by rings of Saturn by Daniel Roseberry (@danielroseberry) for Schiaparelli (@schiaparelli). Custom couture sari and trail by Sabyasachi (@sabyasachiofficial). Custom jewellery by Sabyasachi Fine Jewellery (@sabyasachijewellery). Ring Bhavya Ramesh (@bhavyarameshjewelry). Shoes Christian Louboutin (@louboutinworld). Glasses by Anna Karin Karlsson (@annakarinkarlssonofficial). Styling Anaita Shroff Adajania (@anaitashroffadajania). Make up Kabuki (@kabukinyc). Hair Angelo Seminara (@angeloseminara_hair). Nails Sylvie Macmillan (@sylviemacmillan.nails). Draping Dolly Jain (@dolly.jain): pp.32, 54, 55; National Gallery of Modern Art, New Delhi: p.18; National Institute of Design Archives, Ahmedabad. Photo PM Dalwadi: pp.10, 152; Naushad Ali. Photo Rema Chaudhary: pp.61, 62, 81; Naushad Ali. Photo Ashish Shah: pp.72, 80; nilaHOUSE Jaipur, Lady Bamford Foundation: p.145, p.164t, p.165t; nilaHOUSE Jaipur, Lady Bamford Foundation. Photo Gourab Ganguli: p.180t; NORBLACK NORWHITE. Photo by team NORBLACK NORWHITE: p.45; NORBLACK NORWHITE. Photo Bharat Sikka: p.124; NORBLACK NORWHITE. Photo Bhavya Ahuja of NORBLACK NORWHITE: pp.44, 46–47; NORBLACK NORWHITE. Photo Bikramjit Bose: pp.123, 134–135, 196–197 P: © Pamela Singh, courtesy of sepiaEYE: p.126b; Courtesy of Paiwand. Photo Arka Patra: pp.176, 177; Payal Khandwala. Photo The House of Pixels (@thehouseofpixels). Hair and makeup Krisann Figueiredo (@krisann.figueiredo.mua). Talent Aditi Mishra (@aditi_mishra18), Samruddhi Shirodkar (@__Samruddhiii): pp.86– 87; Payal Khandwala. Photo Soujit Das (@soujit.das). Hair and makeup Chriselle Ann Baptista (@chrissybaps). Talent Vibha Mehta (@13moondust): p.60; Payal Khandwala. Photo Soujit Das. Hair and makeup Mruganayanee (@mruganayanee). Talent Priyadarshini Chatterjee (@priyadarshini.96): p.85; Photo Pranjal Gupta: p.14; Photo Prarthna Singh: pp.165b, p.180b; Photo Pulkit Mishra: p.111 R: Photo © Raghu Rai/Magnum Photos: pp.130–131; Photo © Randhir Singh: p.113; Courtesy of Rashmi Varma. Photo Mehak Narang: p.84; Photo Ravi Choudhary/Hindustan Times. © 2017 Hindustan Times: p.138, 139t; Raw Mango. Photo Ashish Shah: pp.48t, 52, 53, 147, 190, 191, 207; Raw Mango. Photo Ritika Shah: p.49; Raw Mango. Photo Shubham Lodha: pp.1, 48b, 51; Reliance A&T Fashions Pvt. Ltd: pp.157, 174, 181; Rimzim Dadu. Photo Dwaipayan Mazumdar. Talent Palak Gupta: p.189; Photo and styling Rishabh (@rishabhad). Clothes Raw Mango: p.112; Photo robertharding/Alamy Stock Photo: p.91 S: Courtesy of Sabyasachi: p.33; Courtesy of Sanchit Art. Photo © Christie's Images/Bridgeman Images: p.19; San Francisco Museum of Modern Art, Foto Forum purchase. Photo Don Ross. Copyright © 2023 Succession Raghubir Singh: p.74; Photo Sara Hylton/Redux/eyevine: pp.100, 102, 103; Photo courtesy of The Sher-Gil Archives & PHOTOINK: p.31; Photo Sidney B. Felsen. © 1975 Sidney B. Felsen: p.149; Studio Medium. Photo Kirti Virmani. Creative direction Dhruv Satija & Riddhi Jain: p.77; Studio Medium. Photo Kirti Virmani. Talent Parvesh Mudgal. Creative direction Dhruv Satija & Riddhi Jain. Stylist James Lalthanzuala. Hair & makeup Shivani Joshi: p.76; Courtesy of Sufiyan Ismail Khatri: p.169t, p.170b; © Sunil Gupta. All rights reserved, DACS 2023. © Charan Singh, courtesy of sepiaEYE: p.101; © Sunil Gupta. All Rights Reserved, DACS/Artimage 2023. Image courtesy of the artist and Hales Gallery, Materià Gallery, Stephen Bulger Gallery and Vadehra Art Gallery: pp.104–105 V: VegNonVeg. Photo Eshaan George: p.175 Y: Yale Center for British Art, Paul Mellon Collection, New Haven: p.143

Acknowledgements

This book was published in conjunction with the exhibition *The Offbeat Sari* at the Design Museum, London, 19 May to 17 September 2023.

Conceived and curated by
Priya Khanchandani

Associate Curator
Rashmi Varma

Assistant Curators
Lara Chapman and Tiya Dahyabhai

Exhibition Project Manager
George Newing

Exhibition Coordinator
Alice Bell

Exhibition Design
Studio MUTT

Graphic Design
Sthuthi Ramesh

The Design Museum would like to thank the following participants for their generous contribution to the exhibition and the wider events programme: Abhinit Khanna, Abraham & Thakore, Abu Jani Sandeep Khosla, Advait, Advaya (House of Angadi), AKAARO, ALOK, Amit Aggarwal, Anamika Khanna, Anavila, Aparna Rao, Apurva Kulkarni, *Architectural Digest*, Arti Sandhu, ASHDEEN, Ashwini Narayan, Bend It Networks, Bharti Kher, Bodice, Border&Fall, Condé Nast, Daniya Kanwal, David Zwirner, Dhruv Dhody, Diksha Khanna, Diya Basu, Doh Tak Keh, Domino Recording, Ekaya Banaras, Ekta Rajani, Eshna Kutty, Estate of Alice Neel, Estate of Raghubir Singh, Gulabi Gang, Hargila Army, Hemang Agarwal, Himanshu Verma, *Hindustan Times*, HUEMN, Imperial War Museum, India Hobson, *India Today* Group, Kiran Nadar Museum of Art, Koshy Brahmatmaj, Kumari, Kynat Salim, Lionsgate, Little Shilpa, Maison Schiaparelli, Mamta Sharma Das, Manish Malhotra, Manou, Mina Malik, Mithu Sen, *Motherland Joint Ventures* Pvt. Ltd., Museum of Art & Photography Bengalaru, Nalli Silks, Natasha Poonawalla, National Gallery of Modern Art New Delhi, nilaHOUSE, Nisha Seneviratne, NORBLACK NORWHITE, Oorbee Roy, Paiwand Studio, Péro, Perrotin, PHOTOINK, *Platform* Magazine India, Prarthna Singh, Priya Ragu, Pulkit Mishra, Raghu Rai, Randhir Singh, Rashmi Varma, Raw Mango, Rimzim Dadu, Rishabh, Royal Ontario Museum, Sabyasachi, Samiksha Agarwal, Samir Rana, San Francisco Museum of Modern Art, Sana Javeri Kadri, Saree Sneakers, Sargam Sethi, Satya Paul, Sher-Gil Archives, Sher-Gil Sundaram Arts Foundation, Shyama Sasidharan, SIDR Craft, Sobia Ameen, Studio Medium, Sufiyan Ismail Khatri, Sunil Kant Munjal, Taanbaan, Tanaya Das, Tanomi Yamamura, Tarun Tahiliani, TATA CLiQ LUXURY, Tazin Mashruba, Unknown Fields Division, VegNonVeg, *Vogue India*, Warner Music, Weavers Studio Resource Centre, Wild Beasts.

END PAGES   Raw Mango, Shekhawas Sari, Moomal collection, 2020; Munsif Molu, 2019. Elizabeth Mech Boro wearing hand-woven molten chevron blue, aqua green and gold metallic saris by AKAARO

Design Museum Publishing
Design Museum Enterprises Ltd
224–238 Kensington High Street
London W8 6AG
United Kingdom

First published in 2023
© 2023 Design Museum Publishing

978-1-872005-64-5

Publishing Manager
Mark Cortes Favis

Project Editor
Cecilia Tricker-Walsh

Editor
Priya Khanchandani

Editorial Assistants
Tiya Dahyabhai and Stefano Mancin

Picture Researcher
Nikos Kotsopoulos

Copyeditor
Simon Coppock

Proofreader
Ian McDonald

Indexer
Nic Nicholas

Designer
Sthuthi Ramesh

Artworker
Chris Benfield

Many colleagues at the Design Museum
have supported this book, and thanks go
to them all.

Distribution
UK, Europe and select territories
around the world
Thames & Hudson
181A High Holborn
London WC1V 7QX
United Kingdom
thamesandhudson.com

USA and Canada
ARTBOOK | D.A.P.
75 Broad Street, Suite 630
New York, NY 10004
United States of America
www.artbook.com

Printed and bound in the UK by
PurePrint